Cambridge Vocabulary for IELTS

Classroom vocabulary practice

PAULINE CULLEN

CAMBRIDGE
UNIVERSITY PRESS

University Printing House, Cambridge CB2 8BS, United Kingdom

Cambridge University Press is part of the University of Cambridge.

It furthers the University's mission by disseminating knowledge in the pursuit of education, learning and research at the highest international levels of excellence.

www.cambridge.org
Information on this title: www.cambridge.org/9780521709767

First published 2008
6th printing 2013

Printed in Dubai by Oriental Press

A catalogue record for this publication is available from the British Library

ISBN 978-0-521-70976-7 Edition without answers
ISBN 978-0-521-70975-0 Edition with answers and Audio CD

Contents

Map of the book 2

Introduction 4

IELTS Test summary 6

Unit 1   Growing up 8
Unit 2   Mental and physical development 12
Unit 3   Keeping fit 16
Unit 4   Lifestyles 22
Unit 5   Student life 26
Test One 30

Unit 6   Effective communication 32
Unit 7   On the move 38
Unit 8   Through the ages 42
Unit 9   The natural world 46
Unit 10   Reaching for the skies 52
Test Two 56

Unit 11   Design and innovation 58
Unit 12   Information technology 64
Unit 13   The modern world 68
Unit 14   Urbanisation 72
Unit 15   The green revolution 78
Test Three 82

Unit 16   The energy crisis 84
Unit 17   Talking business 90
Unit 18   The law 94
Unit 19   The media 98
Unit 20   The arts 102
Test Four 108

Unit 21   Language building 1 110
Unit 22   Language building 2 114
Unit 23   Academic Writing Task 1 118
Unit 24   Academic Writing Task 2 122
Unit 25   General Training Writing Tasks 1 and 2 126
Test Five 130

Recording scripts 132

Wordlist 142

Acknowledgements 148

Map of the book

Unit number	Title	Topics	Test practice
Unit 1	Growing up	Relationships, families and early learning	Listening Section 1
Unit 2	Mental and physical development	The body, the mind	Speaking Part 2 General Training Writing Task 1
Unit 3	Keeping fit	Diet, health and exercise	Academic Reading
Unit 4	Lifestyles	Life, leisure	Listening Section 2
Unit 5	Student life	Study, education, research	General Training Reading Section 2
Unit 6	Effective communication	Language, linguistics	Academic Reading
Unit 7	On the move	Tourism, travel	General Training Reading Section 1
Unit 8	Through the ages	Time, history	Listening Section 4
Unit 9	The natural world	Flora and fauna, agriculture	Academic Reading / General Training Reading Section 3
Unit 10	Reaching for the skies	Space, the planets	Listening Section 3
Unit 11	Design and innovation	Building, engineering	Academic Reading
Unit 12	Information technology	Telecommunications, computers and technology	Speaking Parts 1, 2, 3
Unit 13	The modern world	Globalisation, changing attitudes and trends	Academic Writing Task 1 (describing a chart)
Unit 14	Urbanisation	Problems and solutions, big city life	Academic Reading / General Training Reading Section 3
Unit 15	The green revolution	The environment, climate change and pollution	Academic Writing Task 1 (describing a process)

Unit number	Title	Topics	Test practice
Unit 16	The energy crisis	Natural resources, alternative fuels	Academic Reading
Unit 17	Talking business	Employment, management and marketing	General Training Writing Task 1 Academic Writing Task 2
Unit 18	The law	Crime, punishment	General Training Writing Task 2
Unit 19	The media	The news, fame	Academic Writing Task 2
Unit 20	The arts	Art appreciation, the performing arts	Academic Reading

Reference section		
Unit 21	Language building 1	Using a dictionary, word families
Unit 22	Language building 2	Learning vocabulary, collocation
Unit 23	Academic Writing Task 1	Data, graphs and tables, diagrams and processes
Unit 24	Academic Writing Task 2	Linking words, opinion words, register
Unit 25	General Training Writing	Vocabulary for Writing Tasks 1 and 2

Introduction

What does the book aim to do?

It aims to extend and improve the accuracy of your vocabulary and help you prepare for the IELTS test. It introduces vocabulary through listening and reading texts that reflect the materials used in the IELTS test. Learning new words in context can help you to remember them and also helps you to understand their meaning. This book also gives you opportunities to practise new words so that they can become part of your active vocabulary.

Who is it aimed at?

The book is designed for students working alone who want to revise and extend their vocabulary. But it can also be used as part of an IELTS preparation course in the classroom, or set as homework by a teacher. It is also suitable for advanced students, or those studying English for academic purposes.

What order should I do the units in?

You can work through the teaching units (1–20) in any order, but you should study **all** the units if you want to prepare thoroughly for the test. You may want to start with a particular unit because it relates to a topic in your course book or because you have a particular interest in that area. Units 21 and 22 give helpful tips on learning new vocabulary and how to use a dictionary. These units provide a very useful introduction to learning vocabulary, so it may be a good idea to look at these first.

How do I use the book?

It is best to work through a unit from beginning to end as one exercise may revise the vocabulary from a previous exercise. The test practice sections provide further opportunities to extend your vocabulary, as well as giving you practice in the different sections of the IELTS test.

How are the units organised?

There are 25 units. The first 20 units present and practise vocabulary based on general and academic topics. Each topic is divided into smaller sections. Each unit has three pages of vocabulary exercises based on listening, reading, writing and speaking materials similar to those found in the IELTS test. There is also a focus on pronunciation. In addition, each unit has one page for a test practice activity, or three pages when it is academic reading test practice. The test practice includes examples of all the different tasks in the following papers: Academic Reading, General Training Reading, Academic Writing, General Training Writing, Listening and Speaking (see the summary of the Academic and General Training tests on pp6–7). These tasks provide useful practice and revision even if you are not taking the test.

At the front of the book is a summary of what is in each part of the IELTS test. The last five units of the book provide a general guide to learning and using new vocabulary. Units 21 and 22 give useful tips on developing vocabulary and using a dictionary. Units 23 – 25 focus on useful vocabulary for the different writing sections of the IELTS test. Units 23 and 24 are designed for students planning on taking the Academic Training Module and Unit 25 is designed for students planning on taking the General Training Module. At the end of the book you will also find:

- recording scripts
- wordlists for each unit

What is on the audio CD?

You need to listen to the audio CD to do the listening and pronunciation exercises in each unit. The test practice listening tasks are also on the audio CD. In the IELTS listening test you hear everything once only so try not to replay the track.

How do I use the wordlists?

There is a wordlist for each unit at the back of the book. Some of these words may be specific to one topic area, but many of them can be found and used in a wide variety of contexts. You may want to divide these wordlists up into groups of ten words to learn at a time. It may be a good idea to study the wordlist before you begin each unit. Alternatively your teacher might use the wordlist as a test or review at the end of each unit (or you could ask a friend to do this). You should be able to understand these words when you read or hear them, but you should also try to extend your active vocabulary by using them in your writing and speaking tasks. You should learn the correct spellings of words as well as any words that collocate, or can be used together with them. Use Units 21 and 22 to help you develop good vocabulary learning strategies.

How do I do the writing test practice?

The writing test practice questions give an opportunity to use the vocabulary from the unit. You should focus on organising ideas and using vocabulary accurately and effectively. You will be penalised if you produce a learnt essay in the IELTS test.

How do I do the speaking test practice?

The speaking test practice questions give an opportunity to use the vocabulary from the unit. In part 2 of the speaking test you will be allowed to make notes, so think of any useful vocabulary you could use and write this down to help you as you talk. If possible, you should record your answers and play them back. Consider your pronunciation as well as the words you used. How could you improve your answer? Ask a friend or a teacher for their comments.

When should I do the vocabulary tests?

There are five tests. Each one tests the vocabulary in five units (Test 1: Units 1–5, Test 2: Units 6–10, Test 3: Units 11–15, Test 4: Units 16–20, Test 5: Units 21–25). When you have finished five units, do the test and mark it. Highlight the questions you got wrong and go back to the units you need to look at again. If you are an advanced student then you may want to take the test before you begin the units to see how much you already know. This may help to pinpoint your weak areas so that you can focus on these in the main units (1–20).

When should I use a dictionary?

The aim of the listening and reading activities in each unit is to give you practice in guessing the meaning from context, so you should try to do each exercise without a dictionary first, unless you are instructed to do so. When you have finished, use the *Cambridge Advanced Learner's Dictionary* or another suitable monolingual dictionary to look up any words you don't know. Try to be aware of words that you need to look up more than once. These are obviously key words for you to learn. Write them down with their meanings, together with any example sentences used in the dictionary. A good dictionary will also tell you words that collocate or can be used together with them. It is a good idea to make a note of these as well. Remember

that some words have more than one meaning, so check what the unit or exercise is about to make sure you find the correct meaning. Look at Unit 21 if you need more help on how to use a dictionary.

How do I learn and revise vocabulary?

Some of the vocabulary in a unit will be new to you and some will be words you are familiar with, but cannot yet use accurately. Even if you feel you know a word, you may be making collocation mistakes and using the incorrect preposition or verb, for example. You might like to use a notebook and organise your vocabulary under the following categories:
- New words to learn
- Words I need to use more
- Words I often make mistakes with
- Topic words (e.g. The Environment; Fuel; Energy; Work etc)

Alternatively, you could simply highlight these words using a different colour highlighter for each category: for example, a blue highlighter for topic words, a red highlighter for words you often make mistakes with, and so on.

Units 21 and 22 will help you to develop good vocabulary learning techniques.

IELTS Test Summary

Academic Training Module

Academic Reading (1 hour)

including the time needed to transfer your answers, there is no extra time given for this

There are three reading passages and 40 questions. The texts are authentic and academic in nature. Examples can be found in units 3, 6, 9, 11, 14, 16, 20. Visit the following website for a detailed description of each of the different question types: www.ielts.org

Academic Writing (1 hour)

There are two writing tasks, writing task 1 and writing task 2. You must answer both tasks. Task 2 carries more marks than task 1.

Task	Timing	Length	What do I have to do?	Assessment	Example units
Task 1	20 minutes	150 words	Describe visual information, e.g. a diagram, chart, graph or table.	• Task achievement • Coherence and cohesion • Lexical resource • Grammatical range and accuracy	7, 13, 15, 23
Task 2	40 minutes	250 words	Write a discursive essay. You may be asked to provide a solution, evaluate a problem, compare and contrast different ideas or opinions, or challenge an argument or idea.	• Task response • Coherence and cohesion • Lexical resource • Grammatical range and accuracy	17, 19, 24

Listening (approximately 30 minutes)

plus 10 minutes to transfer your answers to the answer sheet

There are four sections and 40 questions. In the IELTS listening test you will hear the recording ONCE ONLY. Each section is a little more difficult than the one before. The test is divided up as follows:

Section	What will I hear?	Example units
1	A conversation between two people: e.g. finding out information about travel.	1
2	A monologue or prompted monologue on a general topic, e.g. a radio broadcast.	4
3	A dialogue between two or three people in an academic context, e.g. discussing an essay.	10
4	A monologue in an academic context, e.g. a lecture.	8

There are ten questions for each section. Visit the following website for a detailed description of each of the different question types: www.ielts.org

Speaking (11 to 14 minutes)

In the IELTS speaking test you will be interviewed on your own by one examiner. The interview has three separate parts and is divided up as follows:

Part	Timing	What do I have to do?	Example units	Assessment
1	4–5 mins	Answer questions on familiar topics, e.g. hobbies, daily routine.	12	• Fluency and coherence • Lexical resource • Grammatical range and accuracy • Pronunciation
2	3–4 mins	You are given a card with a topic (e.g. describe a good friend) and some suggestions on it. You have up to one minute to make notes. You then talk about the topic for 1–2 minutes.	2, 12	
3	4–5 mins	Answer more abstract questions about the topic, e.g. How important is friendship?	12	

General Training Module

Candidates for the General Training module take the same listening and speaking test as the Academic module. Only the reading and writing papers are different.

General Training Reading (1 hour)

The General Training reading paper has three sections each of increasing difficulty. The sections are organised as follows:

Section	Reading texts	Example units
1	Two or three short texts or several shorter texts, e.g. advertisements.	7
2	Two texts giving factual information, e.g. information about a course. (NB From May 2009 this will change to work-related information.)	5
3	One long text.	9, 14

Visit the following website for a detailed description of each of the different question types: www.ielts.org

General Training Writing (1 hour)

There are two writing tasks. You must answer both of them. Task 2 carries more marks than task 1.

Task	Timing	Length	What do I have to do?	Assessment	Example units
Task 1	20 minutes	150 words	Write a letter in response to a given situation.	• Task achievement • Coherence and cohesion • Lexical resource • Grammatical range and accuracy	2, 17, 25
Task 2	40 minutes	250 words	Write a discursive essay. You may be asked to provide a solution, evaluate a problem, compare and contrast different ideas or opinions, or challenge an argument or idea.	• Task response • Coherence and cohesion • Lexical resource • Grammatical range and accuracy	18, 25

1 Growing up

Relationships, families and early learning

Relationships

1.1 Look at the following topics and decide whether you would discuss them with

A   your family   B   your friends   C   a teacher

1   a study problem   3   buying something expensive

2   your favourite music   4   the last film you saw

1.2 🎧 1a Listen to four people talking about the topics above. Write the number of the topic (1–4) from the list above and the person/people the speakers say they would talk to about this. Write the words that helped you decide.

Speaker	Topic (1–4)	Words that helped you	Person/people they would talk to
A	4	movies, latest releases	classmates
B			
C			
D			

> **Vocabulary note**
>
> Group together words that are similar in meaning or form, e.g. *adulthood*, *brotherhood*, *fatherhood*. NB *hood* is used to form a noun and shows something belongs to a particular group or has reached a particular stage (*adulthood* = the stage of being an adult).

1.3 🎧 1a Listen again and decide which of the speakers (A–D) the sentences apply to.

1   The relationship between my brother and me is very close. ...C...

2   I have a lot more in common with my friends than with my family. ....

3   I have established a close connection with an older member of my family. ....

4   The relationship between my parents and me has broken down. ....

1.4   COLLOCATION Use words and phrases from the recording and the statements in **1.3** to complete the sentences.

1   My sister and I have totally different tastes. In fact we don't have much .... at all.

2   There is a very close .... between a mother and a newborn baby.

3   It is important to .... a good working relationship .... your work colleagues.

4   A relationship can easily .... if you don't work at it.

5   I really admire the relationship .... my mother and my grandmother.

6   There can be a lot of .... between teenagers and their parents.

Families and early learning

2.1 Scan the text below and underline these words:

rewarding   sibling   relate   accommodating   adolescence   interaction   nurture

Study links early friendships with high-quality sibling relationships

Children who experience a rewarding friendship before the birth of a sibling are likely to have a better relationship with that brother or sister that endures throughout their childhood, said Laurie Kramer in a University of Illinois study published in December's Journal of Family Psychology.

'When early friendships are successful, young children get the chance to master sophisticated social and emotional skills, even more than they do with a parent. When parents relate to a child, they do a lot of the work, figuring out what the child needs and then accommodating those needs,' says Kramer. However, this is not usually the case when two children are interacting.

The research showed that the benefits of early friends are long-lasting. 'Children who had a positive relationship with a best friend before the birth of a sibling ultimately had a good relationship with their sibling that lasted throughout adolescence,' Kramer said. 'And children who as preschoolers were able to coordinate play with a friend, manage conflicts, and keep an interaction positive in tone were most likely as teenagers to avoid the negative sibling interaction that can sometimes launch children on a path of anti-social behavior,' she added. 'From birth, parents can nurture and help develop these social competencies (or skills) by making eye contact with their babies, offering toys and playing with them,' she said.

2.2 Read the text and match the words you have underlined to the following definitions.

1   help someone/something develop and grow

    ....

2   agreeing to a demand   ....

3   brother or sister   ....

4   respond to somebody   ....

5   the stage between childhood and adulthood

    ....

6   giving a lot of pleasure   ....

7   communication   ....

> ### Vocabulary note
>
> Look for familiar words in longer words to work out their meaning, e.g. cor**relation** (one thing is linked with another); inter**related** (the relationship between two or more things). NB The prefix co-, (**co**rrelation or **co**operate) often means *with* or *together*. The prefix inter- (**inter**act or **inter**city) often means *between*.

2.3 Read the text again and say whether these sentences are true (*T*) or false (*F*). Underline the part of the text that gave you your answer.

1   If young children have good friends then they will have a good relationship with their brother or sister. ....

2   Parents help their children develop more social and emotional skills than friends do. ....

3   Friends will give you what you want more often than your parents do. ....

4   Teenagers who fight with their brothers or sisters may behave in a way that is socially unacceptable. ....

5   If parents play with their children more then they will learn how to be more sociable. ....

2.4 A lot of words connected with families and relationships can also be used in a different context. Complete the sentences with a word from the box.

adopt	nurture	relationship
conflict	related	relative
family	relation	

1 The wolf is a member of the dog ....

2 The company decided to .... a new approach to staff recruitment.

3 The study found a strong .... between a lack of friends and sibling rivalry.

4 Whether you think the price of goods is high is .... to the amount of money you earn.

5 Studies have shown that stress in adulthood can be .... to an unhappy childhood.

6 Good teachers identify the talents of their students and .... them.

7 This evidence seems to .... with the findings from previous studies.

8 I am writing in .... to the job advertisement in yesterday's paper.

Error warning

Note the following common errors: *I am writing **in relation to/with** your job advertisement.* NOT *in relation of ... . My **relationship with** my parents is very strong.* NOT *My relationship with my parents ...*

V Vocabulary note

Note these collocations with the word *relationship*.
Verbs: ***build** a relationship*, ***develop** a relationship*, ***establish** a relationship*, ***form** a relationship*, ***have** a relationship*
Adjectives: *a **close** relationship*, *a **long-standing** relationship*, *a **working** relationship*, *a **successful** relationship*
Prepositions: *a relationship **with** someone*, *a relationship **between** two things or people* (NOT *relationship to someone*)

3.1 COMPOUND NOUNS Match the words in box A with the words in box B to make 10 compound nouns. You will need to use some words more than once.

A	active	family	maternal	sibling	stable
	extended	immediate	physical	striking	

B	family	instinct	rivalry	upbringing
	gatherings	resemblance	role	

....
....
....
....
....

3.2 🎧 1b Think about your answers to these questions. Then listen to a student's answers and tick the phrases you hear in 3.1.

1 Tell me about your family.

2 Who are you most similar to in your family?

3 What do you think it takes to be a good parent?

3.3 🎧 1b Listen again and find the words that match these definitions.

1 caring and supportive ....

2 the emotional connection between people or places ....

3 similar ....

4 your nature or character ....

5 determined to an unreasonable degree ....

6 handed down through a family ....

3.4 Now practise answering the questions fully. Record your answers, if possible.

Test practice

LISTENING Section 1

 1c

Questions 1–10

Complete the form below using **NO MORE THAN TWO WORDS AND/OR A NUMBER** for each answer.

Ascot Child Care Centre
Enrolment form

Personal details

Family name: .... Cullen ....

Child's first name: (1) ....

Age: (2) ....

Birthday: (3) ....

Other children in the family: a brother aged (4) ....

Address: (5) ...., Brisbane

Emergency contact number: 3467 8890

Relationship to child: (6) ....

Development

- Has difficulty (7) .... during the day
- Is able to (8) .... herself

Child-care arrangements

Days required: (9) .... and ....

Pick-up time: (10) ....

2 Mental and physical development

The body, the mind

The body

1.1 How old were you when you first learned to

A crawl ....
B walk ....
C talk ....

D ride a bike ....
E read ....
F tie a shoelace? ....

1.2 (🔊 2a) You will hear a talk about early development in children. Listen and complete the table below. Write **NO MORE THAN TWO WORDS** for each answer.

Stage	Social and emotional milestones	Physical milestones	Cognitive and communicative milestones
Infant	• likes to mimic • tries to see how parents react to their (1)	• can sit and stand without help	• can use basic words and (2) .... • uses objects for their intended purpose
(3)	• is more (4) .... • takes turns	is able to • run • (5) .... things • ride a tricycle	• greater understanding of language • uses (6) .... in play
Middle childhood	• the (7) .... has a greater impact on development • some children appear grown up, others are (8)	• growth is not as (9) .... as in earlier stages • (10) .... and (11) .... are the same size as in adulthood	• good reading and writing (12) ....

1.3 (🔊 2a) Listen to the talk again and find words that mean the same as the following.

1 learned (a skill) ....
2 copying people ....
3 without help ....
4 in a natural, unforced way ....
5 developed a skill to a high level ....
6 phase (2 words) ....

1.4 WORD BUILDING Complete the table.

Verb	Noun	Adjective
develop		
grow		fully-
		mature

2.1 Read this text about development in adolescence. Then complete the following sentences with words from the text.

The final stage before adulthood is adolescence. This is a period of transition for teenagers and there are many crucial milestones. Socially and emotionally, teens worry that they may not be developing at the same rate as their peers. They become extremely self-conscious and may be overly sensitive about their appearance. Teens may rebel against their parents but are also more able to accept the consequences of their actions.

This is also a period of enormous physical change and adolescents experience changes in their physical development at a rate unparalleled since infancy. These changes include significant gains in height and weight. Within a year, boys and girls can gain an average of 4.1 inches and 3.5 inches in height respectively. This growth spurt typically occurs two years earlier for girls than for boys and can tend to make both sexes go through a clumsy phase. In terms of their cognitive development, adolescents have greater reasoning skills and have developed the ability to think logically and hypothetically. They are also able to discuss more abstract concepts. They should also have developed strategies to help them study.

1 First-year students often struggle with the ....*transition*........ from high school to university.

2 The .... at which a change occurs can cause problems for both the very young and the elderly.

3 It can be less stressful to make a presentation to your .... rather than to your teachers.

4 The increase in violence among young people may be a .... of watching too much violence on TV and in video games.

5 Petrol prices are increasing at a speed that is .... since the oil crisis of the 70s.

6 Teenagers .... rebel against their parents between the ages of 14 and 16.

7 In part three of the speaking test you are expected to be able to talk about more .... topics.

8 Infinity is a very difficult .... for children to grasp.

2.2 What stage would you associate the following words and phrases with? Write the words in the correct column below.

crawling   immature
irresponsible   nurturing
overindulgent   overprotective
patient   rebellious
throw a tantrum   tolerant
unsteady

Childhood	Parenthood
clumsy	mature

Vocabulary note

The prefix *im-* is often in front of adjectives beginning with *b*, *m* or *p* to form the opposite or to show that something is lacking: **im**mature, **im**possible. Similarly, *ir-* often comes in front of words beginning with *r*, *il-* often comes in front of words beginning with *l* and *in-* in front of other words: **ir**responsible, **il**legal, **in**sensitive. However, there are exceptions: unbelievable, displeased, unlikely, unpopular etc. The prefix *over-* can also be negative, meaning too much: overdeveloped, overdue, overcrowded, oversensitive.

Error warning

Grow can be used with plants: *We could grow flowers and trees here.* Or with things: *The business is growing rapidly.* But *grow up* can only be used with people or cities: *The city grew up from a small group of houses near the river. Grow up* is intransitive, which means you can't use it with an object. NOT ~~The government grew up the city.~~

2.3 Many words used to talk about human growth can also be used to talk about data and statistics. Complete the sentences with a suitable word from the text in 2.1. You may need to change the form of the words.

1 The p.............................. of greatest stability occurred between 1985 and 1990.

2 The greatest period of g.............................. was in 2004.

3 The figures g.............................. from 2,500 to 6,000 in 2007.

4 The company g.............................. an extra 2,000 employees in 2002.

5 Sales increased at a significant r.............................. between 2001 and 2005.

6 The number of migrants rose s.............................. from 1980 to 2000.

The mind

3 Match the phrases in A with the definitions in B.

A		B	
1	keep an open mind	A	increase your knowledge
2	bear in mind	B	I forgot
3	have something in mind	C	I couldn't remember a thing
4	have something on your mind	D	remember
5	my mind went blank	E	try not to judge before you know the facts
6	it slipped my mind	F	be worried about something
7	put your mind at ease	G	have an idea
8	broaden the mind	H	stop you from worrying

4.1 Think about your answers to these questions.

1 What do you remember about your early childhood?

2 Do you think you have a good memory or a poor memory?

4.2 🎧 2b Now listen to a student answering the questions in 4.1 and make a note of all of the words and phrases connected with memory.

remember, memories, ...

....

....

....

Error warning

Remember = to have a memory in your mind. I **remember** my first day at school.
Remind = someone or something helps you to remember something. Remind is not usually used with the subject I. It reminds me of when I lived in Egypt. NOT I remind of when. You remind me of my sister. NOT I remind me of.

4.3 Correct the vocabulary mistakes in these sentences.

1 I will always memory how beautiful the sunset was on that day. ....remember.........

2 I have very fond reminders of my school days. ....

3 Could you remember me to buy some bread on the way home? ....

4 At school we always had to memory long lists of vocabulary. ....

5 I remind how happy our childhood was. ....

Test practice

Speaking Part 2

Describe a memorable period or event from your childhood.

You should say:
- **what the event or period was**
- **what happened during this event or time**
- **why it was memorable and what you learned from this experience.**

You will have to talk about the topic for 1–2 minutes. You have one minute to think about what you are going to say. You can make notes if you wish.

Test Tip

Answer the question as fully as possible. Time yourself to see if you can talk for two minutes. Remember that you will be given up to one minute to prepare for this part of the test. You can make notes if you want, but you don't have to. Use the prompts on the card to give you ideas and help you plan your answer.

....
....
....
....
....
....

General Training Writing Task 1

You should spend about 20 minutes on this task.

Finding it hard to remember important facts and figures? Improve your memory in 10 weeks with our Memory Course. Places are limited and the course is available for only a short time.

Apply in writing to:

Test Tip

Make sure that you address all the points in the question. Organise your ideas before you start to write and when you have finished, check your spelling and the number of words you have used.

You see the above advertisement for a course designed to help improve your memory.
Write a letter to the organisers of the course. In the letter
- **give some background information about yourself**
- **explain your own problems and why you would like to do the course**
- **enquire about the methods used on the course**
- **enquire about course fees and dates.**

You should write at least 150 words. You do not need to write any addresses.

You should begin your letter

Dear Sir or Madam

3 Keeping fit

Diet, health and exercise

Diet

1.1 **Answer these questions.**

1 How healthy are you?   A very healthy   B moderately healthy   C unhealthy?

2 Tick the appropriate column below to show how often you eat the different foods.

I eat ...	at least once a day	a few times a week	once a week	rarely / never
cakes or chocolate				
fried fast foods				
fish				
fruit				
meat				
vegetables				

1.2 **Complete the gaps in the text below using words from the box.**

factors   ingredients   maintain   nutrients   overeating   overweight   servings   variety

How to improve your diet

- Make sure that you eat a (1).............................. of foods. It is important to eat from all five food groups.
- Eat plenty of fruit and vegetables. These contain vital (2).............................. and leading dietitians recommend eating at least two (3).............................. of fruit and three of vegetables every day.
- Try to (4).............................. a healthy weight. Being too thin can cause as many health problems as being (5).............................. Remember, the correct weight for you depends on many different (6).............................. including your age, height and sex.
- Eat moderate portions and don't be tempted to order a larger size when eating out. Skipping meals can lead to (7).............................. as you will be much hungrier later, so be sure to eat regularly if you want to curb your appetite.
- You don't need to eliminate all of your favourite foods but do check the (8).............................. on food labels and make sure that you reduce your intake of foods that are high in fats, sugar and salt.
- If you have a food allergy, make sure you avoid any of the ingredients that can trigger an attack.

1.3 **Match these words and phrases with words from the advice in 1.2.**

1 very important ....

6 limit ....

2 food scientists ....

7 desire to eat ....

3 neither small nor large ....

8 totally remove ....

4 servings ....

9 a condition that causes illness if you eat certain foods ....

5 missing out on ....

10 activate ....

Health and exercise

2.1 **3a** You will hear part of a health
talk. Listen and complete the summary below.
Write NO MORE THAN TWO WORDS.

The heart is a (1)............................... . A diet high
in (2).............................. can slow down the
(3).............................. and lead to heart
problems. A heart attack is caused when an
artery that (4).............................. to the heart becomes (5).............................. . Patients must be given
(6) .... immediately. A stroke is caused when there is a blockage in an artery that leads to the
(7).............................. . A stroke can have a major effect on your body and as yet there is no (8) ....
A healthy diet will keep your arteries (9) .... and can lower the (10) .... of a stroke
or heart attack.

> ### Vocabulary note
>
> The following words are often used with the word *health*.
> Nouns: *health **benefits**, health **risks**, health **problems**,
> health **care**, health **education**, health **system***
> Adjectives: ***in good** health*, ***in poor** health*, ***in excellent**
> health*
> We can use *healthy* to describe things other than your
> body: *a healthy **appetite**, a healthy **diet**, a healthy **economy**,
> a healthy **disrespect for authority***

2.2 **3b** Now listen to part 2 of the talk and answer the questions.

1 Write down three types of aerobic exercise that are mentioned: ....

2 Listen again and find words that mean the same as
the following:

A in a fixed pattern ....*regular*............

B quickly ....

C little by little ....

D a strong suggestion ....

E speed ....

F doing something to excess ....

G get better ....

H every second one ....

> ### Error warning
>
> Note that *health* is a noun and *healthy* is the
> adjective. We write or talk about *education and*
> **health** or *mental* **health**. NOT ~~education and healthy~~
> or ~~mental healthy~~. We say someone is *strong and*
> **healthy** NOT ~~strong and health~~

> ### Vocabulary note
>
> *-tion* at the end of a word usually indicates that the
> word is a noun: ac*tion*, repeti*tion*.
> *-tious* indicates an adjective: repeti*tious*

3 WORD BUILDING Complete the table below. You
do not need to write anything in the shaded areas.
Write the opposites where indicated (*opp.*).

Noun	Verb	Adjective
allergy		
benefit		
harm		
		opp. =
health		
		opp. =
infection		
	opp. =	

Noun	Verb	Adjective
nutrition		
		obese
	prevent	
		recommended
variety		

4.1 PRONUNCIATION (🎧 3c) Put the words into the correct box according to their sound, then practise saying the words. Listen and check your answers.

bath, bathe, birth, breath, breathe, death, growth, health, mouth (v), mouth (n), teeth, teethe, writhe

θ (an unvoiced sound as in **th**ink)	ð (a voiced sound as in **th**is)
bath	bathe

4.2 (🎧 3d) Complete the sentences with words from 4.1. Then listen to the recording to check your answers. Practise saying the sentences.

1 I took a deep .... before diving into the water.

2 The baby is crying because he's .... He got two new .... only yesterday.

3 Old people should take care of their ....

4 He's been so happy since the .... of his son.

5 The pain was so bad she was .... in agony.

6 He can't .... You need to get him to hospital.

5 Improve this essay by replacing the words in *italics* with ONE OR TWO words from this unit.

In the future we won't have to worry about what we eat. We'll just take a tablet to give us all that our body needs and cooking will become a thing of the past.

In our modern world we often look for quick solutions to our problems. We expect to be able to achieve a great deal with little effort. But I don't believe we can apply this notion to our diet and still remain healthy. Preparing a healthy meal can take a lot of time. First you need to have fresh ingredients. Pre-packaged foods can contain a lot of unhealthy additives and so they are not as [1] *good for your body* as fresh food. You also need to make sure to include a [2] *lot of different* foods to make sure that you receive all of the vitamins and minerals that are [3] *very, very important* to a healthy diet. It is not surprising then that some people want to find a simple solution to this in the form of a pill. Fast foods are very high in fat, sugar and salt and so we should eat them in small amounts. For some people, however, these foods have become their staple diet and as a result they are [4] *fat*. If we want to [5] *stop* this from becoming an even bigger problem in the future then we need to address this situation now. While vitamin tablets may be of some benefit, they are unlikely to be effective in the fight against [6] *people getting too fat*.

Health authorities need to increase public awareness of these issues, but we also need to be realistic. Fast food is popular not only because it is convenient but also because it is tasty. Perhaps we should [7] *strongly advise* that people who eat fast food every day should at least [8] *swap* fast food with fresh food *on every second day*. Finally, we eat for pleasure as well as nutrition and for this reason I believe that pills will never replace well-cooked food.

1 ....nutritious.......   3 ....   5 ....   7 ....

2 ....   4 ....   6 ....   8 ....

6 Answer the questions. Write one or two sentences.

1 Do you think young people are more or less fit than 50 years ago? (Why? / Why not?)

....

2 In what way is your diet different from when you were a young child?

....

3 What changes do you think will occur in our diet in the future?

....

Test practice

Academic Reading

Read the following passage and answer questions 1–14.

The causes, diagnosis and prevention of stress

In prehistoric times, the physical changes in response to stress were an essential adaptation for meeting natural threats. Even in the modern world, the stress response can be an asset for raising levels of performance during critical events such as sports activities, important meetings, or in situations of actual danger or crisis. If stress becomes persistent and low-level, however, all parts of the body's stress apparatus (the brain, heart, lungs, vessels and muscles) become chronically over- or under-activated. This may produce physical or psychological damage over time. Acute stress can also be harmful in certain situations.

Psychological effects of stress

Studies suggest that the inability to deal with stress is associated with the onset of depression or anxiety. In one study, two-thirds of subjects who experienced a stressful situation had nearly six times the risk of developing depression within that month. Some evidence suggests that repeated release of stress hormones disrupts normal levels of serotonin, the nerve chemical that is critical for feelings of well-being. Certainly, on a more obvious level, stress diminishes the quality of life by reducing feelings of pleasure and accomplishment, and relationships are often threatened.

Nevertheless, some stress may be beneficial. For example, although some research has suggested that stress may be a risk factor for suicide (a 2003 study found a higher risk for suicide in women reporting both low and very high stress), those with moderate stress levels had the lowest risk.

Heart disease

The effects of mental stress on heart disease are controversial. Stress can certainly influence the activity of the heart when it activates the sympathetic nervous system (the automatic part of the nervous system that affects many organs, including the heart). Such actions and others could theoretically negatively affect the heart in several different ways.

Nevertheless, evidence is still needed to confirm any clear-cut relationship between stress and heart disease. For example, a 2002 study in Scotland found no greater risk for actual heart disease or heart events even in men who reported higher mental stress. In fact, higher stress was associated with fewer heart events, although men with high stress levels did tend to complain of chest pain and to go to hospital for it more often than those with lower stress levels.

Evidence has linked stress to heart disease in men, particularly in work situations where they lack control. The association between stress and heart problems in women is weaker and there is some evidence that the ways women cope with stress may be more heart-protective. In one study, for example, men were more apt than women to use alcohol or eat less healthily in response to stress than women, which might account for their higher heart risks from stress. Different stress factors may affect genders differently. In one study, work stress was associated with a higher risk for heart disease in men, but marital stress – not work stress – was associated with more severe heart disease in women with existing heart problems.

Eating problems

Stress can have varying effects on eating problems and weight. Often stress is related to weight gain and obesity. Many people develop cravings for salt, fat and sugar to counteract tension and, thus, gain weight. Weight gain can occur even with a healthy diet in some people exposed to stress. In a 2000 study, lean women who gained weight in response to stress tended to be less able to adapt to and manage stressful conditions. The release of cortisol, a major stress hormone, appears to promote abdominal fat and may be the primary connection between stress and weight gain in such people.

In contrast, some people suffer a loss of appetite and consequently lose weight. In rare cases, stress may trigger hyperactivity of the thyroid gland, stimulating appetite but causing the body to burn up calories at a faster than normal rate. Chronically elevated levels of stress chemicals have been observed in patients with anorexia and bulimia. Some studies, however, have not found any strong link between stress and eating disorders.

Pain

Chronic pain caused by arthritis and other conditions may be intensified by stress. However, according to a study on patients with rheumatoid arthritis, stress management techniques do not appear to have much effect on arthritic pain. Some studies have clearly linked job dissatisfaction and depression to back pain, although it is still unclear if stress is a direct cause.

Tension-type headaches are frequently associated with stress and stressful events. Some research suggests that headache sufferers may actually have some biological predisposition for translating stress into muscle contractions.

Sleep disturbances

The tensions of unresolved stress frequently cause insomnia, generally keeping the stressed person awake or causing awakening in the middle of the night or early morning. In fact, evidence suggests that stress hormones can increase during sleep in anticipation of a specific waking time. However, there is some hope for sufferers in this area as relaxation therapy has been found to reduce stress levels and consequently improve the quality of sleep.

Test Tip

True / False / Not Given questions – *False* means that the information in the question is factually wrong. *Not Given* means that the information in the statement is impossible to check because it is not mentioned in the text. Use the questions to help guide you through the reading passage. Look for clues in the questions to find the correct part of the passage then read this section carefully.

Questions 1–4

Do the following statements agree with the information given in the passage?
Next to questions 1–4 write

True	if the statement agrees with the information in the passage
False	if the statement contradicts the information in the passage
Not Given	if there is no information on this

1 Stress was originally an important way of keeping humans safe. ....

2 If stress continues for a long time, all of the body's organs are affected. ....

3 The study into the psychological effects of stress involved people with a history of depression. ....

4 Increased stress causes the body to produce more serotonin. ....

Questions 5–6

Choose the correct answer A, B, C or D.

5 The 2003 study into the link between stress and suicide found that
    A fewer women suffer from stress than men.
    B stress reduces the risk of suicide in some women.
    C a larger number of men commit suicide than women.
    D women with low stress levels are less likely to commit suicide.

6 In 2002, a Scottish study showed that

    A there is a strong link between stress and heart problems.

    B there is a link between high stress levels and hospital visits.

    C a reduction in stress would reduce the risk of heart attacks.

    D men with high levels of stress felt no physical symptoms.

Test Tip

For *classification* items, locate the part of the text which refers to the three options you are given. Read this part of the text carefully and look for ideas that match the ideas in the questions. Remember, the wording will not be the same as in the question!

Questions 7–9

Classify the following characteristics as being associated with

A only men

B only women

C both men and women

Write the correct letter A, B or C next to questions 7–9.

7 There may be a variety of causes of stress. ....

8 Their way of dealing with stress can protect the heart. ....

9 Increased heart disease is linked to stress at home. ....

Questions 10–13

Classify the following characteristics as being associated with

A pain

B weight

C sleep

Write the correct letter A, B or C next to questions 10–13.

10 The problem is reduced if stress is lowered. ....

11 An increase in the severity of this problem may be related to work. ....

12 Stress may cause levels to increase or decrease. ....

13 This problem may be the result of the body's natural reaction to stress. ....

4 Lifestyles

Life, leisure

Life

1.1 Think about how you would answer the following questions.

1 Do you think people work too much nowadays?

2 What do you like to do to relax?

3 What is your idea of a perfect day?

4 How would you describe your attitude to life?

1.2 🎧 4a Now listen to four people answering these questions and decide which of the words in the box best describes each speaker.

pessimist   realist   optimist   risk-taker

Speaker 1 ....

Speaker 3 ....

Speaker 2 ....

Speaker 4 ....

1.3 🎧 4a Listen to the speakers again and complete the following phrases.

Speaker 1	work hard for .... ; .... something in life; life has its ....
Speaker 2	live life on .... ; feel .... ; your quality ....
Speaker 3	have a .... attitude; life is full of ....
Speaker 4	have a positive............................. ; live life to .... ; .... a happy life

1.4 Make a note of any of these words and phrases that apply to you and then answer the questions in 1.1 again.

....

....

....

2 COLLOCATION **Complete the words or phrases in the sentences with *life* or *living*. Which answers are written as one word?**

> ### Vocabulary note
>
> Note the difference between *life* and *living*. *Life* is used to refer to the period between birth and death, *living* is used to refer to being alive, *make a living* refers to earning money.

1 Going to Egypt and seeing the pyramids was a *once in a* .... *time* opportunity for me.

2 The *standard of* .... in my country is very good; there are not many poor people there.

3 In my job as a nurse I get to meet people from *all walks of* ....

4 For me, being a vegetarian is not just about diet, it has become *a way of* ....

5 Many people only think about bills they need to pay and forget to allow for everyday .... *expenses* when they calculate a budget.

6 It was a .... *long* ambition of mine to travel to the Arctic Circle and see the northern lights.

7 A rise in petrol prices inevitably leads to a rise in the *cost of* ....

8 The happiest people are those who have found a way to *make a* .... from their hobby.

Leisure

3.1 **Read the text and decide whether the sentences below are true or false. Match the words in bold in the sentences with one of the underlined words or phrases in the text.**

'Leisure activity isn't just for fun,' says a University of Florida psychologist who has developed a scale that classifies hobbies based on needs they satisfy in people. The scale can help people find more personal fulfilment by giving them insight into what they really like. 'The surprising thing is that activities you might think are very different have similar effects on people,' said Howard E.A. Tinsley, a UF psychology professor who developed the measurement. 'Probably no one would consider acting to have the same characteristics as roller-skating or playing baseball, but men and women who act as a hobby report feeling an intense sense of belonging to a group, much the same way others do in playing sports.'

And activities providing the strongest sense of competition are not sports, but card, arcade and computer games, he found. Participating in soccer satisfies our desire for a sense of 'belonging' and coin collecting and baking fulfil their need for 'creativity'. 'With so many people in jobs they don't care for, leisure is a prized aspect of people's lives,' Tinsley said. 'Yet it's not something psychologists really study. Economists tell us how much money people spend skiing, but nobody explains why skiing really appeals to people. Or how one activity relates to another, perhaps in unexpected ways,' Tinsley said. 'Fishing, generally considered more of an outdoor recreational activity, for example, is a form of self-expression like quilting or stamp collecting, because it gives people the opportunity to express some aspect of their personality by doing something completely different from their daily routine,' he said.

1 Both acting and roller-skating give people a **strong feeling** of being part of a team. ....True – intense sense..........

2 **Taking part** in sports gives you the strongest **desire to win**. ....

3 Collecting things **satisfies people's desire** for **making things**. ....

4 Researchers already know why a hobby **attracts** a person. ....

5 Fishing allows you to show the **type of person you are**. ....

3.2 Now look at the remaining words and phrases that have been underlined in the text and match them to these definitions.

1 a feeling of doing what you have always wanted to do ....

2 a deep understanding ....

3 a feature of ....

4 something that is done for enjoyment in your free time. (x3) ....

5 things you do every day ....

4.1 COLLOCATION Match the verbs with nouns from the box. You may use the words more than once.

achieve ⟨ .... *a goal* ....
           .... *a balance* ....

           .... *a living* ....   play ....

make ⟨   ....   put   ....

           ....   set   ....

           ....

meet   ....   take ⟨ ....
                                                           ....

miss ⟨   ....
           ....

a need	a goal
a balance	a living
a choice	a role
a change	an opportunity
a chance	pressure (on)
a decision	

4.2 Correct the 14 vocabulary mistakes in the text.

Although we have a better standard of living nowadays, in many ways our quality of life is not as good as in the past because we are always too busy to enjoy what we have.

Everyday life today is much more complicated than in the past. Even in our leisure time we have to ~~take~~ so many choices about what to do or even what to watch on TV. We are often spoilt for choice and this can leave us feeling confused and dissatisfied. We all know that it is important to get a balance between work and play, but many of us do not succeed. Instead, we make extra pressure for ourselves by trying to be as successful in our work life as in our personal life.

Life in the past was much simpler as many people worked to get their basic needs. Today, for many of us, our job is not just a way of making a life. For many, work is an important role in our everyday life and gives us a strong sense of personal fulfilment. What is more, we have become much more materialistic. Many people get themselves goals such as buying a new house or car and so we measure our success by the material things we own. Desiring these luxuries is what motivates us to work much harder than in the past, so in many ways we choice this way of life.

We have worked hard to improve our standard of living, but it may have come at a very high price. We need to take some changes in our priorities so that family occasions are as important as business meetings. We should also make every possible opportunity to relax and enjoy our leisure time. Once you have given the decision to do this, you should find that your quality of life also improves. My ultimate aim is to have a happy family life. If I get this goal then I know I will not regret any chances I have lost to stay longer at the office.

1 .... *make* ....   6 ....   11 ....

2 ....   7 ....   12 ....

3 ....   8 ....   13 ....

4 ....   9 ....   14 ....

5 ....   10 ....

Test practice

Listening Section 2

 Questions 1–10

Complete the notes using NO MORE THAN ONE WORD AND/OR A NUMBER for each answer.

Things to do in the holidays
- Main problem – children do not have a traditional **(1)**............................... .

Some ideas
- Give children jobs, for example cleaning the **(2)**............................... .

- At home, ask children to help in the **(3)**............................... .

- Get children to make **(4)**............................... ahead of time.

- Get children involved in community work such as visiting the **(5)**............................... .

- Involve older children in long-term **(6)**............................... in your community.

- You may get some ideas from the **(7)**............................... .

- The local **(8)**............................... is often the best place to find ideas.

Things to remember
- Make sure children stay **(9)**............................... .

- Children up to the age of **(10)**............................... need to be supervised by an adult.

---

5 Student life

Study, education, research

Study

1.1 Before you read the text, answer these questions.

1 Do you prefer to study
   A at school or college B in a library C at home?

2 Do you study best
   A early in the morning B during the day C at night?

3 Do you prefer to work
   A with friends B with background music C in silence?

1.2 Now complete the text with the correct form of the verbs in the box. There may be more than one possible answer so try to use each verb once only.

| concentrate | do | learn | overcome | organise | study | take | teach | review | revise |

Even the most studious among you will probably have difficulty studying at some stage in your academic career. If or when this happens, the only way to (1)......................... this problem is to go back to basics. First, make sure you have a comfortable environment to (2)......................... in. Some students need to have a quiet space to themselves and can't (3)......................... if there are too many distractions. Others need some sort of background noise, such as music or the company of friends. Whatever your personal preference is, you need to (4)......................... this first of all. Next, make sure you have all of the equipment or tools that you need. For example, if you are (5).........................a geography course and you have to (6)......................... about countries and their capital cities then you will need to have your atlas to hand. If you're (7)......................... your maths homework then be sure to find your calculator, ruler, protractor and compass before you start. Perhaps you're not preparing a homework assignment or project, but are trying to (8)......................... for an exam. If so, you need to know exactly what is on your curriculum. You should also (9)......................... your notes and make sure that you have a clear understanding of what your lecturers have (10)......................... you. Of course, people with a learning disorder such as dyslexia may need to work harder than others at their studies as they often struggle to read even relatively simple texts.

1.3 Now read the text again and find a word or phrase to match these definitions.

1 describes someone who studies a lot ....

2 things that stop you from working ....

3 a sound you can hear, but do not actively listen to ....

4 two different types of homework or school task .... and ....

5 to study for an exam ....

6 another word for *syllabus* ....

7 to check your work ....

8 to do something with great difficulty ....

1.4 Underline the correct words in each sentence.

1 I would really like to <u>*learn about*</u> / *study about* the ancient Egyptians.

2 We need to *find out* / *know* where to buy the tickets for the concert.

3 I got into trouble at school because I didn't *know* / *find out* my multiplication tables.

4 I did well in the test because I had *known* / *learned* how to spell all of the words on the list.

5 Excuse me, do you *find out* / *know* where the nearest post office is?

6 It was difficult for me to *learn* / *study* at home, because we didn't have a lot of space.

7 I want to *learn how* / *study how* to drive a car.

8 I think you can only really *learn from* / *learn with* experience.

> ### Error warning
>
> *Know* = already have the information; *find out* = get the information.
> *Study* = learn about a subject through books / a course: *I'm studying law; I'm studying for my exams.* We don't use any other prepositions after *study*. NOT ~~I am studying about law.~~
> *Learn* = get new knowledge or skills: *I'm learning English; I'm learning to knit.* Note that we say you are *taking a course*, NOT ~~learning a course.~~
> NB Prepositions after *learn*: *learn about, learn from, learn to*: *I learned a lot from this course.* NOT ~~I learned a lot with this course.~~

Education

2.1 (5a) Replace the words in *italics* below with ONE word. Then listen to the recording and check your answers.

Teacher Can you tell me about your early education?

Student Well, I went to [1] *a school for very young children* from the age of four and I remember that I didn't enjoy it very much at all. My [2] *from the age of 5 to 11* school was a little better, especially because my mum was a teacher in the school. She taught in the [3] *younger part of the* school and she was actually my teacher in first [4] *level*, but when I went up to the [5] *older part of the* school I didn't see very much of her. After that I was lucky enough to receive a [6] *chance to go to school without paying fees* for a very good [7] *from age 11 to 18* school. My parents couldn't have afforded to send me to a [8] *not free* school so it was a really great opportunity for me. It was a [9] *only for one sex* school, so there were no boys. I'm glad I didn't go to a [10] *for boys and girls* school because I think there are fewer distractions so everyone can just concentrate on their studies.

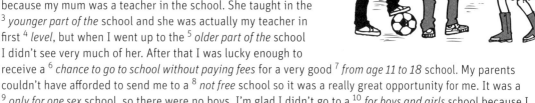

1 ...kindergarten...   6 ....

2 ....   7 ....

3 ....   8 ....

4 ....   9 ....

5 ....   10 ....

> ### Vocabulary note
>
> Words ending in *-ist* are usually used to describe a person who studies a particular subject or who holds a particular set of beliefs: *economist, scientist, feminist, Marxist*.

2.2 WORD BUILDING Complete the table.

Subject	Person	Adjective
architecture		
		archaeological
biology		
economics		
geology		
	geographer	
	journalist	
languages		
	lawyer	
		mathematical
science		

2.3 Complete the sentences with suitable words from the table.

1 I've always wanted to go on an ....archaeological.... dig to try to find fossils and ancient artefacts.

2 Have you seen a copy of the a............................... plan for the new building?

3 My daughter is a l...............................; she speaks six different languages.

4 The government has a good e............................... policy. I'm sure the recession will be over soon.

5 I'm studying j..............................., I've always wanted to be a political writer.

6 I'm not very familiar with the g............................... of that part of the world.

Research

3.1 ⓐ 5b You will hear part of a talk for students. Listen and complete the notes below. Write NO MORE THAN TWO WORDS for each answer.

Continuing your studies *after graduation*
Writing your *dissertation*

Important considerations:

• Many students struggle to find a research
  (1)............................... .

• Writing a (2)............................... *is easier* if you make the right choice.

You need to:

• Study the (3)............................... .

• Have a *wide* (4)............................... of your *field of study*.

• *Establish* what is (5)............................... in your field.

• Have a clear idea of the (6)............................... of your study.

• *Consider* whether there are any (7)............................... in existing research.

• *Think about* your (8)............................... carefully.

• Ask about (9)............................... from outside sources.

  Ask your (10)............................... to check your *results*.

3.2 ⓐ 5b Listen to the talk again and write synonyms for the words in italics in **3.1**.

after graduation = postgraduate,
....
....
....
....
....
....
....

4 PRONUNCIATION ⓐ 5c Mark the stress on these words. Then listen and check to see if you were correct. Practise saying the words.

acad**e**mic	assignment	consideration
concentrate	controversy	conduct (v)
distraction	dissertation	economist
educational	educated	research (n)
thesis	theory	theoretical

Test practice

General Training Reading Section 2

Work experience and internship programs

Through our student work experience program, the education authority provides over 9,000 work experience placements for young people each year. Our program is designed to offer employment opportunities for students that will enrich their academic studies and help them gain valuable work-related skills thereby improving their chances of finding a good job after graduation. A placement does not need to be related to a particular field of study and so participants may even discover areas of work they have never considered before.

All secondary and post-secondary school students in full-time education are eligible to apply for the program. Individual case managers will determine the minimum level of academic achievement required for each job. During an academic term, a student may work part-time. During the summer holidays a student may work full-time or part-time. The education authority is responsible for the recruitment of all students under the work experience program. Applicants apply in person to our office and we refer candidates to the appropriate department.

Our internship program is designed specifically for post-secondary students, whether part-time or full-time. Students on the internship program are given an assignment related to their research area offering them the chance to use their academic knowledge in an actual work setting. The academic institution plays an important role in the placement of students under this program and they will determine the duration of a work assignment. These traditionally last four months but internship assignments may vary from 4 to 18 months. Students in this program normally work full-time.

Questions 1–3

Complete the sentence with the correct ending **A–E**.
Write the correct letter, A–E, next to questions 1 – 3.

1 You can apply for the work experience program ......

2 You can work on the student work experience program full-time ......

3 You can only join the internship program ......

A	if you have high academic results from your educational institution.
B	if you are a full-time student.
C	outside of normal term time.
D	when you have graduated from university.
E	if you have finished your secondary education.

Questions 4–8

Complete the summary below.
Choose **NO MORE THAN TWO WORDS AND / OR A NUMBER** from the text for each answer.

To take part in the work experience program, first you need to apply to the **(4)**.................................... . Your **(5)**.................................... will tell you what qualifications you need. The internship program allows undergraduates to gain work experience in their **(6)**.................................... . The maximum length of an internship assignment is **(7)**.................................... . This is decided by the **(8)**.................................... .

Test Tip

The information in the summary may not be in the same order as in the reading text.

Test One (Units 1–5)

Choose the correct letter A, B, C or D.

1 My company has .... a new approach to staff meetings. We now have them standing up!
   A adapted   **B** adopted   **C** addressed   **D** admitted

2 You can tell a lot by the way members of a family .... with each other.
   A identify   **B** interact   **C** relative   **D** understand

3 We were unable to reach an agreement because of the .... between the two groups.
   A contact   **B** concern   **C** connection   **D** conflict

4 If we don't .... the artistic skills of young children they are far less creative as adults.
   A nurture   **B** nature   **C** provide   **D** prevent

5 There is a very clear relationship .... education and academic success.
   A about   **B** between   **C** for   **D** in

6 I have a very close relationship .... with my mother.
   A to   **B** with   **C** of   **D** for

7 The .... to make quick decisions is vital in an emergency.
   A ability   **B** knowledge   **C** skill   **D** talent

8 In my country people use their hands and .... a lot when they talk.
   A show   **B** tell   **C** gesture   **D** imitate

9 I have very fond .... of my time in Spain.
   A memorise   **B** minds   **C** souvenirs   **D** memories

10 Children need to learn to accept the consequences .... to their actions.
    A of   **B** or   **C** in   **D** by

11 My older brother is very .... for his age. He still needs my parents to help him with everything.
    A mature   **B** maturity   **C** immature   **D** immaturity

12 Everyone should travel; it really .... the mind.
    A broadens   **B** develops   **C** opens   **D** widens

13 I can't eat peanuts because I'm .... to them.
    A allergy   **B** allergic   **C** appetite   **D** infection

14 Some forms of this disease are .... and can last for five years or more.
    A chronic   **B** acute   **C** moderate   **D** obese

15 Unfortunately, scientists have been unable to find a .... for this complaint.
   A prevention   **B** disorder   **C** therapy   **D** cure

16 The man was put into an isolation ward because the disease was highly ....
   A infected   **B** infectious   **C** harmful   **D** harmed

17 After several hours the doctor was finally able to give us his .... John had broken his ankle.
   A diagnosis   **B** disease   **C** symptoms   **D** signs

18 Eating fatty foods can damage your ....
   A healthy   **B** health   **C** harmful   **D** unhealthy

19 You can't always play it safe. Sometimes you need to .... a risk.
   A have   **B** make   **C** put   **D** take

20 It's important to set yourself clear .... so you know what you are aiming for.
   A ambitions   **B** goals   **C** decisions   **D** opportunities

21 She is very .... All she cares about is clothes and expensive cars.
   A realistic   **B** optimistic   **C** materialistic   **D** pessimistic

22 I like making things with my own hands. It gives me a lot of ....
   A satisfaction   **B** exhaustion   **C** fulfilment   **D** creation

23 I always try to keep a positive .... on life.
   A overview   **B** overlook   **C** outlook   **D** insight

24 The cost of .... has risen dramatically in the last few years.
   A life   **B** live   **C** lives   **D** living

25 The researchers .... many experiments to find the most effective materials.
   A confirmed   **B** conducted   **C** considered   **D** concerned

26 Children who do not learn to read before they finish .... school struggle throughout the rest of their education.
   A primary   **B** first   **C** nursery   **D** kindergarten

27 My tutor has some very interesting .... on how students learn.
   A topics   **B** thesis   **C** themes   **D** theories

28 We had to cancel the project due to lack of ....
   A findings   **B** funding   **C** limits   **D** controversy

29 We had to cover the rest of the .... ourselves while our teacher was ill.
   A contents   **B** current   **C** syllable   **D** syllabus

30 I can already speak three languages, but I'd really like to .... to speak Chinese.
   A know   **B** study   **C** learn   **D** teach

6 Effective communication

Language, linguistics

Language

1.1 Which of the following aspects of English do you find the most difficult?

A vocabulary   B grammar   C reading   D writing

E pronunciation   F speaking   G listening

1.2 🔊 6a Listen to somebody talking about learning a language and say which THREE things in **1.1** she had difficulty with.

....

1.3 🔊 6a Listen again and find words that match these definitions.

1 change words from one language to another ....

2 the ability to do something without making mistakes ....

3 something that prevents successful communication ....

4 a person who has spoken the language from birth ....

5 the ability to speak without hesitation ....

6 work or carry out daily tasks ....

2.1 IDIOMS 📖 Use a dictionary to check the meaning of the phrases in the box. Then complete sentences 1–8 with the correct phrase.

| There is something to be said for | You can say that again! | having said that | have a say |
| When all is said and done | Needless to say | That is to say | to say the least |

1 **Bill** Hello, Sam, what a surprise meeting you here!
   Sam .... !

2 Nuclear power has its problems. However, ..., many people believe it is the energy source of the future.

3 .... switching to solar energy, although it is still too expensive for many people.

4 Life without a constant supply of water can be difficult, ...

5 ...., there is little we can do to save the environment without the full support of industry and the government.

6 The tanker spilled 5,000 megalitres of oil into the ocean. ...., this had a devastating effect on marine life in the area.

7 There is a clear link between humans and environmental problems. ...., wherever humans live, they damage the environment in some way.

8 I think it's important for everyone to .... in how the government is elected.

Error warning

Note the following common errors with *say*, *speak*, *talk*, *tell*.
I speak German. NOT ~~I talk German.~~ *She's always **talking about** her dog.* NOT ~~tell about.~~ *Can I **tell you** something?*
NOT ~~tell something.~~ NB Tell can be used to refer to a chart /graph: *The chart **tells** us how many students were enrolled.*
However, it is better to use language that is more impersonal: *The chart **shows** how many students were enrolled.* NB
You should not use *say* to talk about charts: ~~From the chart I can say how many students.~~

2.2 Correct the mistakes in these sentences.

1 The chart ~~talks~~ us how many students were studying in the college in 1990. ....*tells*..........

2 I can't understand what he is speaking. He's almost incoherent. ....

3 Today I'm going to tell about my last holiday in America. ....

4 I can talk three languages fluently, but Italian is my mother tongue. ....

5 I learned English from a textbook, so I don't really understand it when it is said. ....

6 The table says the percentage of people moving into urban areas between 1960 and 1990. ....

2.3 The words in column B should be similar in meaning to those in column A.
Cross out the odd word in each group.

A	B			
communicate	contact	correspond	~~indicate~~	interact
1 conclude	close	summarise	recap	recall
2 explain	clarify	define	express	illustrate
3 mean	indicate	intend	signify	stutter
4 meaning	conjecture	connotation	significance	sense
5 say	demonstrate	express	speak	verbalise
6 suggest	imply	intimate	propose	state
7 tell	gesture	narrate	recount	relate
8 understand	appreciate	comprehend	contradict	follow

Linguistics

3.1 Read the text and then answer the questions.

Signs of success
Deaf people are making a profound contribution to the study of language

Just as biologists rarely see a new species arise, **linguists** rarely get to discover an unknown **dialect** or even better, to see a new language being born. But the past few decades have seen an exception. Academics have been able to follow the formation of a new language in Nicaragua. The catch is that it is not a spoken language but, rather, a sign language which arose **spontaneously** in deaf children.

The thing that makes language different from other **means** of communication is that it is made of units that can be combined in different ways to create different **meanings**. In a spoken language these units are words; in a sign language these units are **gestures**. Ann Senghas, of Columbia University, in New York, is one of the linguists who have been studying the way these have gradually **evolved** in Nicaraguan Sign Language (NSL).

The language **emerged** in the late 1970s, at a new school for deaf children. Initially, the children were instructed by teachers who could hear. No one taught them how to sign; they simply worked it out for themselves. By conducting experiments on people who attended the school at various points in its history, Dr Senghas has shown how NSL has become more **sophisticated** over time. For example, **concepts** that an older signer uses a single sign for, such as rolling and falling, have been unpacked into separate signs by youngsters. Early users, too, did not develop a way of **distinguishing** left from right. Dr Senghas showed this by asking signers of different ages to **converse** about a set of photographs that each could see. One signer had to pick a photograph and **describe** it. The other had to guess which photograph he was **referring** to.

When all the photographs contained the same elements, merely arranged differently, older people, who had learned the early form of the language, could neither signal which photo they meant, nor understand the signals of their younger partners. Nor could their younger partners teach them the signs that indicate left and right. The older people clearly understood the concept of left and right, they just could not **express** it. What intrigues the linguists is that, for a sign language to emerge spontaneously, deaf children must have some **inherent** tendency to link gestures to meaning.

3.2 Say whether the following statements are true or false. Give an explanation for each answer using words from the text. Then use your dictionary to check the meaning of any words in bold that you do not know.

1 Ann Senghas studies languages.
   True – she's a linguist.

2 Teachers taught the Nicaraguan deaf children how to use sign language.

3 The earliest form of the sign language was very basic.

4 The older signers were able to show the difference between left and right.

5 Linguists believe that deaf children are born with the ability to link gestures to meaning.

4.1 Think about your answers to these questions.

1 What do you need to do to be a good language learner?
2 What do you think makes a good language teacher?
3 What problems do people experience when they learn your language?

4.2 6b Look at these answers to the questions in 4.1 and complete them with a suitable word from this unit. Listen to the recording to check your answers.

1 Well, you need to be able to put down your textbooks from time to time and forget about (1).............................. . That's the only way to become more (2).............................in a language. You also need to (3).............................. to (4).............................. speakers of the language as much as you can.

2 I think the best language teachers are those who can (5).............................. another language themselves. They also need to be able to (6).............................. things clearly and in a way that is easy to (7).............................. .

3 My (8).............................. language is very difficult to learn because of the (9).............................. . The individual sounds are very strange to other nationalities and difficult for them to (10).............................. .

Test practice

Academic Reading

First words

There are over 6, 000 different languages today, but how did language evolve in the first place?

Pinpointing the origin of language might seem like idle speculation, because sound does not fossilise. However, music, chit-chat and even humour may have been driving forces in the evolution of language, and gossip possibly freed our ancestors from sitting around wondering what to say next.

There are over 6,000 different languages today, and the main language families are thought to have arisen as modern humans wandered about the globe in four great migrations beginning 100,000 years ago. But how did language evolve in the first place? Potential indicators of early language are written in our genetic code, behaviour and culture. The genetic evidence is a gene called FOXP2, in which mutations appear to be responsible for speech defects. FOXP2 in humans differs only slightly from the gene in chimpanzees, and may be about 200,000 years old, slightly older than the earliest modern humans. Such a recent origin for language seems at first rather silly. How could our speechless Homo sapiens ancestors colonise the ancient world, spreading from Africa to Asia, and perhaps making a short sea-crossing to Indonesia, without language? Well, language can have two meanings: the infinite variety of sentences that we string together, and the pointing and grunting communication that we share with other animals.

Marc Hauser (Harvard University) and colleagues argue that the study of animal behaviour and communication can teach us how the faculty of language in the narrow human sense evolved. Other animals don't come close to understanding our sophisticated thought processes. Nevertheless, the complexity of human expression may have started off as simple stages in animal 'thinking' or problem-solving. For example, number processing (how many lions are we up against?), navigation (time to fly south for the winter), or social relations (we need teamwork to build this shelter). In other words, we can potentially track language by looking at the behaviour of other animals.

William Noble and Iain Davidson (University of New England) look for the origin of language in early symbolic behaviour and the evolutionary selection in fine motor control. For example, throwing and making stone tools could have developed into simple gestures like pointing that eventually entailed a sense of self-awareness. They argue that language is a form of symbolic communication that has its roots in behavioural evolution. Even if archaic humans were physically capable of speech (a hyoid bone for supporting the larynx and tongue has been found in a Neanderthal skeleton), we cannot assume symbolic communication. They conclude that language is a feature of anatomically modern humans, and an essential precursor of the earliest symbolic pictures in rock art, ritual burial, major sea-crossings, structured shelters and hearths – all dating, they argue, to the last 100,000 years.

But the archaeological debate of when does not really help us with what was occurring in those first chats. Robin Dunbar (University of Liverpool) believes they were probably talking about each other – in other words, gossiping. He discovered a relationship between an animal's group size and its neocortex (the thinking part of the brain), and tried to reconstruct grooming times and group sizes for early humans based on overall size of fossil skulls. Dunbar argues that gossip provides the social glue permitting humans to live in cohesive groups up to the size of about 150, found in population studies among hunter-gatherers, personal networks and corporate organisations. Apes are reliant on grooming to stick together, and that basically constrains their social complexity to groups of 50. Gelada baboons stroke and groom each other for several hours per day. Dunbar thus concludes that, if humans had no speech faculty, we would need to devote 40 per cent of the day to physical grooming, just to meet our social needs.

Humans manage large social networks by 'verbal grooming' or gossiping – chatting with friends over coffee, for example. So the 'audience' can be much bigger than for grooming or one-on-one massage. Giselle Bastion, who recently completed her PhD at Flinders University, argues that gossip has acquired a bad name, being particularly associated with women and opposed by men who are defending their supposedly objective world. Yet it's no secret that men gossip too. We are all bent on keeping track of other people and maintaining alliances. But how did we graduate from grooming to gossip? Dunbar notes that just as grooming releases opiates that create a feeling of wellbeing in monkeys and apes, so do the smiles and laughter associated with human banter.

Dean Falk (Florida State University) suggests that, before the first smattering of language there was *motherese*, that musical gurgling between a mother and her baby, along with a lot of eye contact and touching. Early human babies could not cling on to their mother as she walked on two feet, so *motherese* evolved to soothe and control infants. *Motherese* is a small social step up from the contact calls of primates, but at this stage grooming probably still did most of the bonding.

So when did archaic human groups get too big to groom each other? Dunbar suggests that nomadic expansion out of Africa, maybe 500,000 years ago, demanded larger group sizes and language sophistication to form the various alliances necessary for survival. Davidson and Noble, who reject Dunbar's gossip theory, suggest that there was a significant increase in brain size from about 400,000 years ago, and this may correlate with increasing infant dependence. Still, it probably took a long time before a mother delivered humanity's maiden speech. Nevertheless, once the words were out, and eventually put on paper, they acquired an existence of their own. Reading gossip magazines and newspapers today is essentially one-way communication with total strangers – a far cry from the roots of language.

Questions 1–5

Choose the correct answer **A**, **B**, **C** or **D**.

1   In paragraph 1, the writer uses the term 'idle speculation' to refer to the study of
  A   why people began to use music.
  B   where language first evolved.
  C   when people began to talk.
  D   how humour first began.

2   What does the writer tell us about FOXP2?
  A   It helps prevent speech problems.
  B   It is the same in chimpanzees as in humans.
  C   It could have first occurred 100,000 years ago.
  D   It could have first occurred 200,000 years ago.

3   In paragraph 2, what notion does the writer refer to as being 'rather silly'?
  A   That language began such a long time ago.
  B   That man could travel around the world unable to talk.
  C   That chimpanzees may have been able to talk.
  D   That communication between chimpanzees pre-dates man.

4   Why does the writer refer to 'lions' in paragraph 3?
  A   To illustrate the type of communication needs faced by early man.
  B   To indicate how vulnerable early man was to predators.
  C   To provide evidence of other species existing at the same time.
  D   To show the relationship between early humans and other animals.

5   Gelada baboons are mentioned in order to show that
  A   using grooming to form social bonds limits the size of a social group.
  B   early humans would probably have lived in groups of up to 50.
  C   baboons' social groups are larger than those of early humans.
  D   baboons spend 40 per cent of their time grooming each other.

Test Tip

For matching items, first locate all the people listed in the text. Read all the
views they express and then find the statement which matches this. NB The
ideas or statements in the questions will not be expressed in exactly the same
words as in the text and they will not be in the same order as in the text. You
may not need to use all of the people in the list.

Questions 6–14

Look at the following statements (questions 6–14) below and the list of people.
Match each statement with the correct person or people, (A–E).
Write the correct letter, **A–E**, next to questions 6–14.
NB You may use any letter more than once.

6   There is physical evidence of increased human intelligence up to 400,000 years ago. ....

7   In the modern world, gossiping is seen in a negative way. ....

8   Language must have developed before art and travel. ....

9   The development of human language can be gauged by studying other species. ....

10   Gossiping makes humans feel good. ....

11   The actions of early humans could have evolved into a form of communication. ....

12   The first language emerged through a parent talking to an infant. ....

13   Gossip was the first purpose of human communication. ....

14   Early humans used language to help them live together. ....

List of people
A   Hauser
B   Noble and Davidson
C   Dunbar
D   Bastion
E   Falk

7 On the move

Tourism, travel

Tourism

1.1 Answer these questions about the place where you live.

1   What would you take a visitor to your hometown to see?

2   Which of the following best describes the place where you live?
    A   coastal   B   mountainous   C   rural   D   urban

1.2 🎧 7a Listen to four people describing where they live and complete the table below. Use the correct adjective from 1.1 for the 'Type of place' column. Write down any words that helped you decide.

Speaker	Type of place	Words that helped you decide
1		
2		
3		
4		

1.3 🎧 7a Listen again and decide which of the speakers' hometowns can be reached:

A   by air ....   B   by rail   C   by road ....   D   by sea ....

1.4 Complete the sentences using the correct form of the words in the box. You may use the words more than once.

| at   low   of   peak   reach   trend   travel   trough |

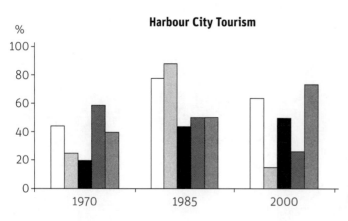

Harbour City Tourism

- city hotel occupancy
- coastal hotel occupancy
- adventure tourism
- rail travel
- air travel

1   The chart shows the .... in tourism in Harbour City in 1970, 1985 and 2000.

2   Adventure tourism rose from a low .... 20 per cent in 1970 to a peak .... 50 per cent in 2000.

3   The occupancy of coastal hotels .... at close to 90 per cent in 1985.

4   In 2000 the number of passengers .... by air .... a peak of 80 per cent.

5   The number of train passengers fell to a .... of approximately 25 per cent in 2000.

6   The two greatest .... occurred in adventure tourism in 1970 and rail travel in 2000.

7   The percentage of coastal hotel occupancy experienced the greatest .... and ....

8   City hotel occupancy peaked .... almost 80 per cent in 1985.

Travel

2.1 **Correct the seven vocabulary mistakes in the text.**

Thanks to modern transport people can now ~~journey~~ a lot more easily than in the past. However, modern-day trip also has its problems: airports can be very crowded and there are often long queues of people waiting to collect their luggages. One way to make this job easier is to tie a colourful ribbon around each of your luggage so they are easier to spot on the conveyor belt. If you are going away on a short journey of only a few days then you may be able to limit yourself to hand luggage and save even more time. For longer travels, make sure you take plenty of snacks and drinks, especially if you are trip with small children.

1   .... _travel_   5   ....

2   6   ....

3   7   ....

4   ....

> ### Vocabulary note
>
> _Travel_ = a verb and an uncountable noun used to talk about travelling in a general way: _Air **travel** has become cheaper than rail **travel** in some places._
> _Trip_ = short holiday or time away: _I have to go on a business **trip** to Japan._ _Trip_ can also be used to refer to a journey. _The bus **trip** was really long._
> **_Journey_** = getting from A to B: _When driving a long way it is best to break your **journey** up into two-hour blocks._
> _Tourism_ = the industry or business of providing holiday transport, accommodation and entertainment.

> ### Error warning
>
> _Travel/Travelling_ = moving from one place to another: _I think **travel/travelling** helps to educate you about the world._ NOT ~~I think tourism helps to educate you~~. NB _Travelling_ = UK spelling, _Traveling_ = US spelling.
> _Luggage_ is uncountable and refers to all of your bags: _Put your luggage/suitcases here._ Not ~~Put your luggages ...~~

2.2 **Think of a suitable word or words to complete the sentences. Then read the following travel advice and check your answers.**

1   I gave my parents a copy of my .... before I left so that they would know where I was.

2   It is difficult to get tickets at that time of year so we booked ours well ....

3   My bank has a lot of branches overseas so I could .... my own account easily.

4   Driving a car during .... periods can be horrendous.

5   Your passport, tickets and money are the only really .... items on any trip.

6   In the duty free shop they asked to see our tickets and some form of ....

7   The exchange rate can .... a great deal, so shop around for the best deal.

8   When we finally reached our .... we were very tired.

Travel advice

The price of holidays can **fluctuate** a great deal throughout the year so try to be flexible with your travel dates and avoid **peak** holiday times. It can also be cheaper if you book well **in advance**. Before your departure, make sure you do as much research about your **destination** as you can. Find out if you require any special visas or permits to travel there. Think about currency as well. Will you be able to **access** your own money easily enough or will you need to take cash with you? Think about eating larger lunches and smaller evening meals to help make your spending money go further, as lunch is generally cheaper. Make sure that you keep sufficient **identification** with you at all times. It may also help to email a copy of your passport details to yourself in case it is lost or stolen. Label your suitcases clearly so that they can be easily identified as yours. It can be useful to store a copy of your **itinerary** in a prominent place in your suitcase so that the airline will know where to find you if your luggage gets lost. Be sure to pack any medication or other **essential** items in your hand luggage. If your flight is delayed or your luggage is lost these can be difficult to obtain in an airport or foreign country.

2.3 Complete the essay below with suitable words from the box. Then, in your notebook, write a conclusion for the essay.

affects	effect	eco-tourism	remote	transport	trend	tourism	tourists

What are the advantages and disadvantages of tourism?

Since the aeroplane became a common form of (1)............................. people have become more adventurous in their choice of holiday destination and expect to be able to fly to even the most (2)............................. parts of the world. But what (3)............................. do tourists have on their surrounding environment?

The arrival of a group of (4)............................. in a small community can mean the end of peace and quiet as they indulge in one long party. When on holiday, away from parents, young people can sometimes change their normal standards of behaviour. Fuelled by alcohol and too much sun they can do damage to themselves as well as the community around them. This invasion (5)............................. the local people in many ways, disrupting their normal routine and increasing their working hours.

However, (6)............................. can also be of benefit to a small community, bringing jobs and a source of income that may not have existed before. This may mean that younger people are encouraged to stay in the community rather than seeking work in the city. There is also a growing (7)............................. towards different types of holidays. Nowadays we hear a great deal about the popularity of (8)............................., which I think indicates that people are more aware of the environment and wish to protect it rather than harm it.

3 PRONUNCIATION ⊙ 7b All of these words contain the letters *ou*, but they are not all pronounced in the same way. Put these words into the correct box according to their pronunciation. Then listen and check.

boundary	bought	cough	course	country	double	doubt	drought	enough
journal	journey	nought	rough	south	southern	tourism	tourist	trouble	trough

ɜː *(as in* bird*)*	ʊə *(as in* pure*)*	ʌ *(as in* cup*)*
journey		
aʊ *(as in* cow*)*	**ɒ** *(as in* not*)*	**ɔː** *(as in* ball*)*

Test practice

General Training Reading Section 1

A

This summer we have a fabulous range of adventure holidays climbing up mountains or flying off them! With our unique all-inclusive formula and budget accommodation, we're sure you will not find better value elsewhere. Our holidays are ideal for young people travelling by themselves as there is no single person supplement and the group lessons included are a great way to meet new people. A minimum age applies to all activities.

B

Discover the hidden beauty of a Roman town and its 21st-century delights. Experience a sumptuous countryside welcome of fine food, admire our world-class heritage and the stunning scenery that surrounds our town. Enjoy the elegance and excitement of our five-star hotel. We offer exclusive couples-only accommodation and you are sure to leave us feeling pampered and relaxed.

C

We offer the widest choice of destinations, accommodation and activities throughout the Alps. We can provide accommodation only or a fully packaged activity holiday including flights and accommodation. As a specialist company we craft tailor-made holidays to your exact needs and specifications. Mountain biking, trekking, skiing and snowboarding are just some of the many activities on offer. We can provide top-quality chalets, hotels or apartments and any combination of the above activities.

D

This Icelandic wonderland never ceases to amaze – with its diverse scenery, wealth of activities and attractions including whale watching and the famous Blue Lagoon, this destination is, not surprisingly, addictive! One of the world's last genuine wilderness areas, this breathtaking, ice-covered landscape is more accessible in the summer than you might think. Forget about hiring a car – why not try rafting along a slow-moving river?

E

This is a captivating holiday destination. There are beautiful beaches, coastal villages, unspoilt coves and bays, clear turquoise waters, breathtaking scenery, mountains that appear to rise out of the sea, cities that sparkle with life, the brilliant sunshine – all contributing to a holiday paradise. There is plenty to see and do and families are particularly well-catered for.

Questions 1–8

Look at the five holiday advertisements, **A–E**.
For which holiday are the following statements true? Write the correct letter **A–E** next to questions 1–8.
NB You may use any letter more than once.

1   Offers both coast and mountains. ....

2   You can observe sea creatures. ....

3   Offers self-catering facilities. ....

4   Good for people travelling alone. ....

5   Offers winter sports. ....

6   Suitable for people with young children. ....

7   Suitable for people with not much money to spend. ....

8   Offers luxurious accommodation. ....

8 Through the ages

Time, history

Time

1.1 **Which of the statements are true for you?**

1 A I wear a digital watch.   B I wear an analogue watch.   C I don't wear a watch.

2 A I write important dates on my calendar.   B I keep a diary.   C I don't use either.

3 A I am very punctual.   B I am often in a hurry.   C I am always late.

1.2 🔊 **8a** **Listen to three people speaking about punctuality and decide whether they are**

A punctual   B always in a hurry   C always late

Speaker 1 ....   Speaker 2 ....   Speaker 3 ....

1.3 🔊 **8a** **Listen again and circle each of the phrases in the box as you hear them. Then complete the sentences below using the correct phrase.**

> on time   in time   took so long   take my time
> the right time   spend time   save time
> lose track of time   time-consuming

1 When I surf the net I often .... Before I know it a few hours have gone by.

2 I try to make my lunch the night before to ....

3 At the weekend I try to .... with my family.

4 I find writing notes by hand very ....

5 We booked a taxi but it .... to arrive that we were 15 minutes late.

6 Excuse me, do you have ....? I have an appointment at 10 o'clock and I really want to get there ....

7 I ran for the bus, but I didn't get there ....

8 I got up very early so that I could .... getting ready.

> **Error warning**
>
> We use *take + time* in the following ways: *Take your time* (= don't hurry), *Take a long time / too much time*. NB We can say *It took a lot of time / so much time / too much time*, but be careful when you use *long: it took a long time / It took too long / It took so long*. NOT *It took too long time / It took so long time.* We can also say *I took three hours to get there* or *It took (me) three hours to get there*.

1.4 **Say whether the words in bold are closest in meaning to *before* or *after*.**

1 Twenty people were injured in the accident and the tower was **subsequently** demolished to prevent it from happening again.

2 **Prior** to the introduction of the steam engine, most people in the UK worked from home.

3 Three years **previously** the government had introduced a new law allowing women to vote for the first time.

4 There was a great deal of excitement in the days **preceding** the election.

5 This is the third year **in succession** that a female has been chosen to manage the club.

6 Istanbul was **formerly** known as Constantinople.

7 I had to pay $2,000 rent **in advance**.

8 The newspapers warned that a stock market crash was **imminent**.

History

2.1 Read the text and then answer the questions below.

🅥 *Vocabulary note*

BC is used in the Christian calendar to refer to the time before the birth of Jesus Christ. *AD* is used to refer to the time after Christ was born. *Circa* is used to mean *about* or *approximately* and is sometimes written simply *c*. NB We do not use an apostrophe to talk about decades: *the 1960s* NOT ~~*the 1960's*~~.

Stonehenge was built over a long period. If we consider only the ancient stones themselves, the work spanned seventy generations – some 1,600 years. However, the first construction at this site began in prehistoric times. True, these first artefacts were just wooden poles which have long gone, but these were raised by men in times so ancient that Britain was still recovering from the Ice Age. The timeline below shows this history, with a frenzy of activity from just before 3000 BC through to 1600 BC being responsible for most of what we now gaze upon in awe.

						Phase 3	
					Phase 2		
postholes					Phase 1		
Ice age ending							
8000 BC	7000 BC	6000 BC	5000 BC	4000 BC	3000 BC	2000 BC	1000 BC

Timeline of the building of Stonehenge

If we consider the structure chronologically, we can see that construction took place in several phases over more than a thousand years. Exact dates are not possible, since dates are inferred from minute changes in physical measurements, such as the radiocarbon dating method. Nevertheless, archaeologists have sketched out the following outline of events. First, the people of the Mesolithic period erected pine posts, known as the postholes, near Stonehenge. In the 1960s a car park was built over these. During the next stage, Phase 1 (c. 3100 to 2700 BC), a ditch was carved into the chalk less than 1 km from Stonehenge. This would have appeared brilliant white in the green of what had now become pastureland as the hunter-gatherers that erected the postholes gave way to farmers. Also during this time the 'henge' (the earthworks; ditch and bank) was constructed. Many visitors to Stonehenge fail to notice the 'henge' since the ditch and bank have been greatly eroded over the passing millennia. In Phase 2 of the construction (c. 2700 to c. 2500 BC), a large number of wooden posts were placed on the site. These may have served as markers for astronomical measurements. We do not know if there are more of them as excavation did not cover a large area. This was followed by Phase 3 (c. 2600 to 2500 BC). Stones began to arrive in this era and the circular shape and pattern of these enormous stones, which predate all other known structures, is still standing today. According to historians, there was no written mention of Stonehenge until 1100 AD.

1 Approximately when was the Mesolithic period? ....

2 What method was used to establish the dates of construction? ....

3 When did the earliest structures become permanently hidden from view? ....

4 What type of people lived at Stonehenge during the Mesolithic period? ....

5 Why do many visitors not see the 'henge'? ....

2.2 Read the text again and find a word or words that match these definitions.

1 an interval of time ....

2 very old ....

3 extended over ....

4 before people made written records of events
    ....

5 arranged in the order in which they actually
    happened ....

6 stage of development ....

7 worn away over time ....

8 thousands of years ....

9 digging for artefacts ....

10 a period of history ....

11 to exist earlier than something else
    ....

2.3 Complete the sentences with suitable words from the box. You do not need to use all of the words. Use a dictionary and make a note of the different meanings in your notebook.

age	ancient	chronological	antique
antiquated		consecutive	era
	the Middle Ages	middle-aged	

> **Vocabulary note**
>
> *Age* = a particular period of history: *the Victorian* **age**, *the digital* **age**. *Era* = a period of time that is remembered for particular events: *The arrival of moving pictures marked the end of an* **era** *for live theatre*. *Middle-aged* = people in their middle years of life: *Most companies are run by* **middle-aged** *men*. *The Middle Ages* = a period of European history between 1000 and 1500 AD.

1 You should organise the dates into .... order from the oldest to the most recent.

2 The museum has an excellent exhibition about life during ....

3 I much prefer studying .... history to modern history.

4 The first moon landing marked the beginning of an exciting .... in space exploration.

5 My grandparents are refusing to adapt to the computer ....

6 It would be better if the meetings were on .... days. We'd get more done that way.

3.1 Answer the questions in your notebook.

1 Do you often think back to the past or do you prefer to concentrate on the future?

2 Do you think it is important for children to study history? (Why? / Why not?)

3 If you could go back in time, which period of time would you like to visit? (Why?)

3.2 Correct the mistakes in *italics* in these answers to the questions in 3.1. Use a dictionary to help you.

1 Yes, I do think about the past almost all ~~times~~, in fact. I think I am a very *nostalgia* person, so I often *look backwards* at my life and remember good times as well as bad. I definitely think about it more than the future.

2 I didn't really enjoy studying history at school. I think teenagers are more interested in *the modern time* than in the past! But now that I'm older, I can see that actually it is very important. We need to know about important *history* events because hopefully they can stop us from making the same mistakes in the future.

3 The *stage* of history I'd most like to visit is ancient Egypt. I think it would be amazing to *go back in times* and watch how they lived and how they built the pyramids. I wouldn't want to stay long though – I think I would miss the digital *period* too much!

1 ...*(of) the time*...
   ....
   ....

2 ....
   ....
   ....

3 ....
   ....
   ....

Test practice

Test Tip

Listen for any plural words and be sure to add an *s* at the end if you need to.
Make sure you check your spelling at the end of the test.

Listening Section 4

 Questions 1–10

Complete the notes below using **NO MORE THAN TWO WORDS AND/OR A NUMBER.**

The history of dentistry

Early history

- The earliest reference to problems with teeth was in (1)............................. .

- The ancient Sumerians called problems with teeth 'tooth (2).............................'.

- There is (3)............................. to show that the Chinese used dental treatments.

Remedies and treatment

- An old text from (4)............................. reveals medical practices from 1700 to 1500 BC. The text refers to the use of (5)............................. and (6)............................. to relieve toothache.

- In the fifth century BC a Greek (7)............................. noted the beginnings of specialisation in medicine.

- A Greek doctor was the first to (8)............................. problem teeth.

- In Europe during the (9)............................., doctors performed dentistry in people's homes.

- A dentist from France is said to have founded (10)............................. dentistry.

---

9 The natural world
Flora and fauna, agriculture

Flora and fauna

1.1 How many plants and animals do you know? Can you name:

A five animals found in Africa?

....

B five different types of flower?

....

C five types of fruit?

....

D five animals found in Australia?

....

E five different types of tree?

....

F five types of vegetable?

....

1.2 Are these words associated with plants or animals? Put the words into the correct column. Which word can go in both columns?

flora   fauna   vegetation   branch   twig   root   coat   predator   beak
trunk   fur   hide   scales   feathers   paw   claw   thorn   petal   horn

Animals	Plants

Error warning

We say we must take care of **nature**. NOT ~~We must take care of the nature.~~ *Natural* is the adjective form: *It is a natural process.* NOT ~~It is a nature process.~~

Which five words in the animal column are connected to their skin or covering?

1.3 COMPOUND NOUNS Complete the sentences by adding one of these words *animal, human, nature, natural* .

1 It's *human* ....nature........ to want to find a solution to our problems.

2 Vegans do not use or eat any .... *products*.

3 I would rather be served by a .... *being* than by a computer.

4 I am constantly amazed by how beautiful and how destructive *mother* .... can be.

5 Man is said to be the most dangerous creature of all the .... *kingdom*.

6 Animals are much happier living in their .... *habitat*.

7 Manmade disasters such as chemical spills can destroy the .... *balance*.

8 In some countries prisoners are denied basic .... *rights*.

1.4 🔊 9a Listen to a description of an animal called a meerkat and complete the table.

Habitat	Diet
• Found in South Africa in (1).............................. areas. • Avoids woodland and thick (2).............................. . • It sleeps in (3).............................. . • If necessary, the meerkat will make a (4).............................. between rocks.	• Meerkats mostly eat (5).............................. , (6).............................. and (7).............................. . • They occasionally eat small rodents and the (8).............................. of certain plants.

Agriculture

2.1 Which is the odd one out? Circle the word which is different from the others and say why.

1   rose tulip daisy (weed) We want to grow the others.
2   plant grow cultivate soil ....
3   crop plant shrub bush ....
4   organic natural chemical biological ....
5   tropical subtropical humid arid ....
6   arid desert semi-arid tropical ....
7   endemic native introduced local ....

2.2 Read the text and then decide if the statements below are true or false. Find words in the text which mean the same or the opposite of the words in bold.

Introduced species

Since the birth of agriculture, farmers have tried to avoid using pesticides by employing various biological methods to control nature. The first method involved introducing a predator that would control pests by eating them. This was used successfully in 1925 to control the prickly pear population in Australia. The prickly pear had originally been used as a divider between paddocks. However, it eventually spread from a few farms to 4 million hectares of farming land, rendering them unusable. The Cactoblastis moth larvae was introduced to help control the situation and within ten years, the prickly pear was virtually eradicated. Further attempts at biological control weren't so successful. When farmers tried to eliminate the cane beetle by introducing the South American cane toad, the results were catastrophic. The cane toad did not eat the cane beetle and the toad population spread rapidly leading to the decline of native species of mammals and reptiles.

1   Farmers do not like using **chemicals to kill pests**. ....
2   The prickly pear was planted as a type of barrier between **fields**. ....
3   The *Cactoblastis* moth **killed off** nearly all prickly pear plants. ....
4   The cane toad was a **native** species to Australia. ....
5   Using the cane toad was **very successful**. ....

2.3 Now read the rest of the text and match the words in *italics* to the definitions below.

Other introduced species have proved similarly *disastrous* among native Australian animals. Since the introduction of the cat, the fox and the rabbit from Europe, 19 species of native animals have become *extinct* and a further 250 species are considered to be either *endangered* or *vulnerable*. The modern-day approach to the biological control of pests is through *genetically modified* crops. It remains to be seen whether this controversial method will have any long-term *repercussions*, particularly in regards to the *ecological balance* of the environment where they are grown. Some fear that insects may *become resistant* to these new crops and therefore become even more difficult to control.

1   at risk ....
2   negative effects ....
3   to stop being affected by something
     ....
4   at risk of dying out ....
5   no longer existing ....
6   crops whose genes have been scientifically changed
     ....
7   extremely bad or unsuccessful ....
8   the relationship between plants, animals, land, air, and water ....

2.4   WORD BUILDING Complete the table. You do not need to write anything in the shaded areas.

Noun	Adjective	Adverb	Verb
agriculture	agricultural		
ecology			
			evolve
	extinct		.... extinct
nature			
	genetic		

3   Improve the text by replacing the words in *italics* with a suitable word or phrase from this unit.

Some farmers believe that growing [1] *fruit and vegetables* that have been [2] *changed so that their genes are different* is a good way to [3] *totally stop* pests and improve the quality of their produce. However, this type of [4] *farming* has both advantages and disadvantages.

One of the advantages is that farmers can grow plants that produce a poison that is harmful to [5] *small animals like flies and caterpillars*. This means that farmers will not have to use [6] *chemicals to kill these animals* and so this should be better for the surrounding environment and the [7] *earth that plants grow in*. As a result, it could help to protect other [8] *plants* as well as the [9] *living space* of any animals in the area.

On the other hand, farmers usually only spray their fields once or twice per year but these new plants would be toxic all year round. Furthermore, it is possible that over time the pests may [10] *stop being killed by* the toxins and so the problem would be worse than ever. The toxins may also be poisonous to other plants and animals and this would upset the [11] *way plants and animals live and grow together* and may lead to more animals becoming [12] *at risk of extinction*.

4   PRONUNCIATION 9b Each of the words in the box below has a weak sound (ə) or *schwa*, e.g. *about*. <u>Underline</u> the schwa in each word, then listen and check your answers. Practise saying the words. There may be more than one schwa in each word.

adapt
agriculture
catastrophe
chemical
climate
disastrous
endangered
genetically
human
natural
vulnerable

Test practice

Academic Reading

Meet the hedgehog

A

In Norwich, England, the first housing development designed for both hedgehogs and people has been built. All through the gardens and fences is a network of pathways and holes installed just for the ancient, spiny creatures. It's a paradise that Fay Vass, chief executive of the British Hedgehog Preservation Society, calls 'absolutely fantastic'. As for the developers, they have reason to think the animals will help make home sales fantastic, too. Part of the attraction is that many people simply love hedgehogs, particularly in Britain, where children's book writer Beatrix Potter introduced Mrs Tiggy-Winkle, a hedgehog character, over a century ago. But part of the attraction is also rooted in science. Studies have helped make clear that hedgehogs are good for gardens, eating vast numbers of slugs and other pests as they forage in the vegetation at night.

Test Tip

This reading text is also good practice for General Training section 3.

B

Recent scientific studies about hedgehogs have helped explain mysteries as varied as why hedgehogs apply saliva to their entire bodies, how they have survived on the planet for 30 million years, why they chew toxic toad skins and what secrets they may hold about evolution. As one of the most primitive mammals on the planet, the hedgehog has been helping geneticists understand evolutionary relationships among mammals and even uncover secrets of the human genome[1]. At Duke University, for example, scientists chose the hedgehog and 14 other species to study the lineages of mammals. They determined among other things that marsupials (e.g. kangaroos) are not related to monotremes (the egg-laying platypus and echidna), which had long been a subject of debate. Such questions are not just academic. 'If you are trying to trace, for example, the evolutionary steps of foetal heart development to better understand how foetal defects occur, it helps to know which mammals are related so that you can make accurate inferences about one mammal from another mammal's development,' says researcher Keith Killian.

C

Still, much about hedgehogs remains unknown. For one thing, scientists think they haven't even discovered all the hedgehog species. 'We know of at least 14,' says hedgehog researcher Nigel Reeve of Britain's University of Surrey, Roehampton. 'It's almost certain that there are more species.' The 14 known species are native to Africa and parts of Asia as well as Europe. Some hibernate through cold winters in the north. Others tolerate desert heat near the equator. Some live in urban areas, adapting well to living in close proximity to humans. Others live in areas that rank among the most remote places on the planet.

D

Hedgehogs spend much of their time alone, but Reeve says it would be a mistake to think of them as solitary. 'Hedgehogs do approach each other and can detect the presence of others by their scent,' he says. 'It is true that they usually do not interact at close quarters, but that does not mean they are unaware of their neighbours. They may occasionally scrap over food items and rival males attracted to a female may also have aggressive interactions. Still, it's fair to say that, in adulthood, hedgehogs meet primarily to mate, producing litters of four or five hoglets as often as twice yearly.'

---

[1] *genome*: the complete set of genetic material of a living thing

E

Adult hedgehogs eat just about anything they can find: insects, snakes, bird eggs, small rodents and more. Veterinarians trying to understand gum disease in domesticated hedgehogs have concluded that the varied diet of wild hedgehogs gives them more than nutrition – the hard bodies of insects also scrape the hedgehogs' teeth clean.

F

All hedgehogs also share the same defence mechanism: they retract their vulnerable parts – head, feet, belly – into a quill-covered ball, using special skin down their sides and over their heads and feet. Any perceived threat can make them roll up, including the approach of a biologist, so researchers have invented a new measurement for the animals: ball length. Young hedgehogs have a few extra defence strategies. 'One is to spring up in the air,' says Reeve. 'A fox would get a face full of bristles. They make a little squeak while they do it.' Evidence suggests that hedgehogs may also add unpleasant chemicals to their quills to make them even less appealing. In behaviour that may be unique for a vertebrate, they chew substances laden with toxins and then apply frothy saliva to their entire bodies. In one 1977 study, human volunteers pricked themselves with quills from hedgehogs that had coated themselves after chewing on venomous toad skins. The volunteers found those quills much more irritating and painful than clean ones.

G

However, every year, many thousands of the animals die on roads in Europe and elsewhere as they go about their nightly business. Along with intensive farming and pesticides, road kill has taken its toll on hedgehog populations. One 2002 study found the animal numbers had dropped by between 20 and 30 per cent in a single decade. To help combat the decline, the British have established special clinics for injured hedgehogs, urged that anyone making a bonfire check for the animals underneath first, and ensured that hedgehogs can cope with cattle grids. Recently, they even persuaded *McDonald's* to alter the packaging of its *McFlurry* ice-cream container, which had been trapping foraging hedgehogs.

H

Ironically, for centuries the English considered these animals as vermin. Even 50 years ago gamekeepers were killing as many as 10,000 a year thinking they were no more than bird-egg-eating pests. In some places today, scientists are coming to the same conclusions all over again. In the 1970s, hedgehogs were introduced to the Hebrides Islands off Scotland to help combat garden slugs. With no natural enemies there, a few hedgehogs soon turned into thousands. Wildlife researchers have watched the hedgehogs reduce the numbers of rare ground-nesting wading birds by feasting on their eggs. Efforts to cull the animals in the past two years have upset Britain's conservationists who have countered with strategies to relocate the animals.

Test Tip

For questions that require you to locate information, you also need to understand the function of the information. For example, for question 1 you will need to find the part of the text which tells you *why* it is important to know how animal species are connected (i.e. the *relevance* of this information).

Questions 1–9

The reading passage has eight sections A–H. Which sections contain the following information? Write the correct letter (A–H) next to questions 1–9 below.

1 The significance of establishing the relationship between different species. ....

2 The different habitats where hedgehogs can be found. ....

3 The reason why standard forms of measurement cannot be used for the hedgehog. ....

4 A problem associated with hedgehogs kept as pets. ....

5 Two reasons why hedgehogs are popular with people in the UK. ....

6 Four findings from the latest research into hedgehogs. ....

7 The social habits of the hedgehog. ....

8 The number of hedgehog species already identified. ....

9 The name given to baby hedgehogs. ....

Questions 10–13

Choose the correct answer A, B, C or D.

10 The study conducted in 1977 revealed a possible reason why
   A hedgehogs clean their quills.
   B hedgehogs chew poisonous animal skins.
   C adult hedgehogs do not leap into the air.
   D young hedgehogs make a high-pitched noise.

11 In Britain, which of the following has NOT been done to protect hedgehogs?
   A The opening of hospitals just for hedgehogs.
   B Imposing fines for littering in areas where hedgehogs live.
   C The alteration of a container produced by a fast-food chain.
   D Alerting people to the potential dangers faced by hedgehogs.

12 What are the 'conclusions' that scientists on the Hebrides Islands have reached again?
   A Hedgehog numbers are declining.
   B Hedgehogs pose a threat to other wildlife.
   C Hedgehogs can safely be introduced there.
   D Hedgehogs can be used effectively as a natural predator.

13 What would conservationists prefer to do on the Hebrides Islands?
   A Introduce a native predator of hedgehogs.
   B Kill a small number of hedgehogs.
   C Remove ground-nesting birds.
   D Move the hedgehogs elsewhere.

10 Reaching for the skies

Space, the planets

Space

1.1 Answer these questions.

1 Would you like to travel into space? (Why? / Why not?)

2 What do you imagine it would be like?

3 What problems do you think you would experience in space?

1.2 Complete the text below with suitable words from the box.

astronauts   atmosphere   commercial   explorers
launch   outer   simulator   weightlessness

If you have ever dreamed of travelling in space then our (1)............................... space travel programme will make that dream a reality. Of course, passengers will need to prepare for this experience. However, unlike the months of training that (2).............................. undergo, our passengers will be ready for (3).............................. within two days. To prepare for a truly out-of-this-world experience, passengers will spend two days in our special training facility. There the passengers will be able to experience zero gravity in a special (4)..............................; this will allow the passengers to acclimatise. During the flight itself a rocket will propel the spacecraft into suborbital space in excess of 100,000 m above the Earth's (5).............................. . This will allow the passengers to experience (6).............................. . Our space (7).............................. will be able to float around the cabin and view the Earth and (8).............................. space for approximately ten minutes prior to re-entry and landing.

1.3 Read the text again and find words that match these definitions.

1 an actual event ....

2 go through an experience ....

3 the force or pull from the Earth ....

4 get used to a change in conditions ....

5 drive something forwards ....

6 more than ....

7 stay up in the air or in water ....

8 entering the Earth's atmosphere again ....

1.4 Complete the sentences with words from the text. You will need to change the form of the words.

1 Some people believe that space e.............................. is a waste of money.

2 Climbing extremely high mountains is made all the more difficult because of the drop in a.............................. pressure.

3 Spacecrafts need to reach extremely high speeds in order to escape the g.............................. pull of the Earth.

4 Last year the astronauts u.............................. a series of mental and physical tests in order to qualify for the mission.

5 This computer program s.............................. extremes of weather so that pilots can experience difficult flying conditions.

The planets

2.1 🔊 10a Listen to someone talking about the problems of forming colonies on other planets. Complete the table with **NO MORE THAN TWO WORDS** from the talk.

Planet	Physical features	Disadvantages
Venus	• same size as 1........................	• has no 2........................ • covered in 3........................ • constant 4........................
Mercury	• smaller than all other planets except 5........................	• has greatest range of temperatures of any planet in the 6........................
Saturn	• has many 7........................ and 8........................	• much too hot

2.2 🔊 10a Listen again and complete the sentences below.

1 Venus is unusual because it .... in the opposite direction to other planets.

2 The .... of Venus has many craters caused by asteroids.

3 Mercury has no substantial ....

4 Mercury does not have any water so cannot .... life.

5 The Voyager space .... has provided us with pictures of Saturn's moons.

6 The .... of Saturn is mainly gas.

2.3 WORD BUILDING Complete the table.

Noun	Adjective
atmosphere	
	cosmic
	galactic
	gravitational
horizon	
	lunar
	meteoric
sun	
	stellar
	terrestrial
universe	

Ⓥ *Vocabulary note*

The suffix *-ic* tells us that a word is an adjective. How many adjectives in 2.3 end in *-ic*? Other common examples are: *economic*, *scenic*, *tragic*.

2.4 Complete the sentences with suitable words from the table in **2.3**.

1 The moon appears much bigger when it is close to the ....

2 The North Star is the brightest star in our ....

3 Many scientists believe that dinosaurs became extinct when a .... hit the Earth.

4 A .... eclipse occurs when the moon is hidden by the sun.

5 Many people wonder if there is intelligent life elsewhere in the ....

6 The teacher told us to draw a .... line across the page.

7 The most successful products in the world are those that have a .... appeal.

8 .... energy is becoming more common nowadays.

3 **Read this news report and decide whether the following statements are true or false. Give a reason for each answer using one of the underlined words in the text. Then check the meaning of any of the underlined words you don't know and write them in your notebook.**

In May 1973, the USA launched its first manned space station. The station, called Skylab, managed to carry three different crews of astronauts over a nine-month period, in spite of the fact that it lost a meteor shield on launch. In February 1974, the final crew returned to Earth and, for the next five and a half years, the Skylab continued to orbit the Earth, unmanned and unused. Its low orbit gradually pulled the 77-tonne Skylab down towards the Earth making a crash landing inevitable and causing a great deal of concern around the world. On 11 July 1979 the Skylab eventually crashed into the southern ocean off Esperance, Australia. Fortunately the debris fell in mostly uninhabited areas and locals scrambled to collect a souvenir. A 17 year-old from Esperance flew to America to claim a $10,000 reward for being the first to deliver a piece of the station to a newspaper. The local council of Esperance issued the USA with a $400 fine for littering. It has never been paid. There are currently approximately 8,000 pieces of space junk floating above our heads thanks to the satellites, space shuttles and space stations out there. One example is a screwdriver lost during a space shuttle mission in 1985 which has never been recovered.

Statements	***True/False***	***Reason***
1 *In late 1974 there were people on board the space station.*	....	*It was* ....
2 *The Skylab may have floated in space for ever.*	....	*A crash was* ....
3 *Very few people lived in the area where it landed.*	....	*The area was* ....

4 **Complete the text using suitable words from this unit.**

'Space belongs to whoever gets there first.' Do you agree with this statement?

Most of (1) p......................... Earth has already been mapped and explored, so it is not surprising that explorers should turn their attention to other parts of the (2) u......................... . The planets in our (3) s......................... s......................... have become the next frontier to be conquered.

We all remember the so-called (4) s......................... race of the 1960s when the US and USSR were each determined to be the first to (5) l......................... on the moon. However, I do not believe that planting a flag on the moon gives anyone the right to claim it as theirs.

With the increasing use of (6) s......................... to monitor activities here on Earth, as well as the very real prospect of space tourism, now is a good time to ask who owns or, more importantly, who governs the vast area of space above us? In the relatively short time that man has been travelling in space we have already left sufficient (7) d......................... behind to show that we are as careless in our space travels as on Earth. The broken shuttle parts have simply been left to (8) f......................... in the atmosphere and cause a very real threat to everyone here on Earth.
Clearly space belongs to all of us. Although there is an international (9) s......................... s .... , this is currently only involved in research. I think we need to act quickly to establish a set of international laws that govern (10) o......................... space.

5 **PRONUNCIATION** 10b **Each of the following words has a weak sound (ə) or schwa, e.g. *about*. Underline the schwa in each word, then listen and check your answers. Practise saying the words. There may be more than one schwa in each word or phrase.**

astronaut atmosphere commercial explorer exploration galaxy
horizon horizontal outer satellite solar system sustain universal

Test practice

Listening Section 3

 10c

Questions 1–4

Choose the correct answer **A**, **B** or **C**

1   According to John, what is the main advantage of space exploration?
    A   To supply resources for use on Earth.
    B   To find out more about the origins of our planet.
    C   To establish a colony for humans if Earth becomes uninhabitable.

2   According to the speakers, why can't robots be sent into space instead of humans?
    A   They cannot operate for long enough.
    B   They are too expensive to build.
    C   They are too reliant on humans.

3   What are we told about the space technology currently used?
    A   It can be unreliable.
    B   It is based on old technology.
    C   It is becoming cheaper to produce.

4   What is the biggest problem in sending robots to Mars?
    A   the distance
    B   the atmosphere
    C   the extreme temperatures

Questions 5–10

Who expresses the following opinions?
    A   John
    B   Susan
    C   Both John and Susan

5   We should plan a trip to Mars even though it may not happen soon. ....

6   We may eventually colonise Mars. ....

7   The soil on Mars is highly toxic. ....

8   The soil on Mars contains materials we could use. ....

9   Spaceships cannot be totally protected from radiation. ....

10   It is possible that humans could form a base on Mars. ....

Test Two (Units 6–10)

Choose the correct letter A, B, C or D.

1 People who are colour blind often can't .... between red and green.
   A see   **B** differ   **C** tell   **D** distinguish

2 Our car broke down twice on the way to the wedding. .... to say we arrived two hours late.
   A Needless   **B** Pointless   **C** Regardless   **D** Worthless

3 I hope the lecturer wasn't referring .... my assignment when he made that remark.
   A in   **B** for   **C** to   **D** of

4 Languages .... over time so dictionaries need to be regularly updated.
   A eliminate   **B** evolve   **C** establish   **D** elicit

5 My teacher said my essay was .... She said she couldn't follow my argument.
   A incompetent   **B** inaccurate   **C** incoherent   **D** incisive

6 It's important to teach children not to .... lies.
   A say   **B** speak   **C** talk   **D** tell

7 These figures .... a peak in 1982 when over 2 million new machines were sold.
   A got   **B** increased   **C** rose   **D** reached

8 Air .... is cheaper than other forms of long-distance transport in my country.
   A trip   **B** journey   **C** travel   **D** travelling

9 A large number of houses were .... by the storm.
   A affected   **B** effected   **C** influenced   **D** involved

10 Many people believe that violent computer games can have a harmful .... on children.
   A affect   **B** effect   **C** damage   **D** involvement

11 The price of fresh fruit and vegetables .... considerably throughout the whole year.
   A rises   **B** peaks   **C** fluctuates   **D** decreases

12 The population of wild birds peaked .... approximately 400,000 before falling rapidly.
   A at   **B** for   **C** in   **D** of

13 My first job was to arrange the files into .... order from the oldest to the most recent.
   A alphabetical   **B** chronological   **C** numerical   **D** historical

14 The train whistle warned us of its .... departure.
   A previous   **B** imminent   **C** subsequent   **D** former

15 The majority of cave art was created in prehistoric ....

    A time   **B** stage   **C** era   **D** times

16 Computer viruses are a modern-..................... problem.

    A day   **B** era   **C** times   **D** time

17 I much prefer life in the twenty-first .... to that of the Middle Ages.

    A age   **B** era   **C** years   **D** century

18 It can take .... time for people to get used to a new system.

    A long   **B** a long   **C** so long   **D** too long

19 Many people are fascinated by the native .... of Australia, especially koalas and kangaroos.

    A fauna   **B** flora   **C** agriculture   **D** vegetation

20 The mother bird carries food back to the nest in its ....

    A feather   **B** wing   **C** beak   **D** paw

21 We must try to protect .... animals, otherwise when a species disappears the whole ecosystem is affected.

    A ecological   **B** endangered   **C** extinct   **D** exotic

22 I believe that farmers should be banned from using .... near waterways.

    A crops   **B** contamination   **C** pollution   **D** pesticides

23 Zoos should try to re-create the animals' .... habitat rather than keeping them in cages.

    A nature   **B** native   **C** natural   **D** naturalist

24 A plant is only as healthy as the .... it grows in.

    A habitat   **B** water   **C** soil   **D** vegetation

25 It must have been amazing to be the first astronauts .... space.

    A in   **B** of   **C** up   **D** to

26 I think we should spend more money taking care of our own ....

    A Earth   **B** atmosphere   **C** planet   **D** stars

27 I think we should spend more on space ....

    A explore   **B** explorer   **C** expansion   **D** exploration

28 Navigation around the globe is a lot simpler thanks to the information we receive from ....

    A satellites   **B** stations   **C** systems   **D** shuttles

29 I don't think we will ever find another planet that can .... life.

    A suspend   **B** survive   **C** supply   **D** sustain

30 I imagine astronauts spend a lot of time thinking about life .... Earth.

    A in   **B** of   **C** down   **D** on

11 Design and innovation
Building, engineering

Building

1.1 **Which adjectives best describe your home?**

A old traditional modern

B concrete brick steel timber

C single-storey two-storey multi-storey / high rise

1.2 **Complete the sentences using the words in brackets in the correct order.**

1 It's a .... house. (brick, traditional)

2 I live in a .... apartment. (high-rise, lovely)

3 I'd rather live in a .... cottage. (small, country)

1.3 **Now make a similar sentence about your own home.**

I live in .... but I'd rather live in ....

> ### 🅥 *Vocabulary note*
>
> If we use more than one adjective they are normally in the following order: opinion, size, age, shape, colour, origin, material, type: An *ugly, old, brown, plastic shopping* bag. However, more than four adjectives together can sound awkward. NOT ~~An ugly, big, old, rectangular, brown, Italian, plastic bag.~~

2.1 🌐 11a Listen to three people describing their homes and complete the table below.

	Type of building	*Material(s) used*	*Favourite feature*	*Adjectives used to describe it*
A				
B				
C				

2.2 🌐 11a Listen again and answer the questions. Include the words from the recording that give you your answers.

Speaker A

1 Where did the stone come from?

....

2 What makes the ceilings ornate?

....

3 Is the house large or small?

....

Speaker B

1 Is the computer system new or old?

....

2 What makes the apartment functional?

....

3 Are the bedrooms large or small?

....

4 Are the buildings around it tall?

....

Speaker C

1 Is this house different from those around it?

....

2 Which room does the speaker say is bright?

....

3 What shape is the bottom of the staircase?

....

We say that you *build a house / a hospital* etc, NOT ~~build a building~~. *Build up* is not used to talk about construction. It refers to increasing or developing something: *He went to the gym to **build up** his muscles. We are trying to **build up** a relationship with a company in Japan. I had to **build up** the confidence to apply for the manager's job.* NOT ~~We need to build up a hospital.~~

Engineering

3.1 Scan the article and underline these words.

invented   hoisted   hauling   platforms   storage   steel   lift shaft   tension
   trigger   device   internal   frame   construction   skyscrapers   landmarks

The elevator

Next time you are in a lift, look for the name of the people who made it. Chances are it will be the Otis Elevator Company. It was Elisha Otis who invented the gadget that made the modern passenger lift possible. The concept of elevation was already well established. Louis XV of France disliked stairs so much that he was regularly hoisted skywards in a 'flying chair' by several strong men hauling on ropes. In Otis's time, warehouses commonly used moving platforms to transport goods between floors. However, elevating anything further than one floor or weighing more than 70 kilograms would have been considered far too dangerous.

Otis worked for a bed manufacturer who was keen to expand his business but needed to find a way to move his beds to an upper floor for storage. The inventive Otis soon had a solution to the safety problem: a tough steel spring system that meshed with ratchets on either side of the lift shaft so that if the rope gave way the sudden loss of tension would trigger the device, stopping the lift from falling.

At the 1854 World Trade fair in New York, Otis unveiled his invention and orders began to pour in, including one from the United States Assay Office which at that time was constructing one of the first buildings with an internal steel frame to support the exterior walls. This was the same construction method that skyscrapers would use. If not for lifts, the towering landmarks which feature so prominently in today's architecture would have been impossible and the character of our cities would be entirely different.

3.2 Decide if the following statements are true or false. Write the words you have underlined that helped you.

1 Elisha Otis came up with the idea that made elevators safe for people. True (invented = came up with the idea)

2 Louis XV was lifted into the air by men pulling ropes. ....

3 Warehouses in Otis's time used boxes to move their goods to different levels. ....

4 Otis's boss wanted to move beds to a higher level for delivery. ....

5 Otis made his springs out of plastic. ....

6 The ratchets were located on the inside of the lift. ....

7 If a rope became slack this activated the contraption. ....

8 The US Assay Office building had its support structure on the outside. ....

9 The US Assay Office used a similar building technique to today's tall buildings. ....

10 The writer believes that skyscrapers can help you find your way around a city. ....

3.3 Match the verbs (1–8) in column A with the definitions (A–H) in column B.

A	B
1 condemn	A build something on a piece of land
2 demolish	B build again
3 develop	C repair and make new again
4 devise	D knock down
5 maintain	E live in or use a space
6 occupy	F judge a building not to be safe
7 reconstruct	G keep in good condition
8 renovate	H invent

3.4 Choose the correct words.

1 We can't move into the house until they have *developed / renovated* it.

2 No one has been allowed to occupy the building since it was *condemned / reconstructed*.

3 The architect *devised / demolished* a clever way of keeping the house cool in summer.

4 The tenants were offered a reduced rent if they agreed to *maintain / occupy* the property.

3.5 WORD BUILDING
Complete the table.

Noun/person	Verb	Adjective or past participle
builder / building	build	
		constructed
	design	
engineer		
innovation		
	invent	
	occupy	
structure		

3.6 Complete the text with words from 3.5.

A group of (1)i............................. architecture students has won this year's Timber Bridge Competition. The students' (2)d............................. beat 17 others. The team used an (3)i............................. approach to their bridge which was (4)b............................. entirely out of timber. They used traditional (5)c............................. methods to avoid using nails or screws. The students demonstrated a good knowledge of fundamental (6)e............................. principles. They (7)c............................. a working model of the bridge, which (8)o............................. an entire car park. This allowed them to test the bridge and ensure that the (9)s............................. was sound.

4 PRONUNCIATION ⏵ 11b Tick the correct sound for each of the letters underlined. Listen and check your answers, then practise saying the words correctly.

1	design	s	z	6	housing	s	z
2	please	s	z	7	fasten	s	z
3	device	s	z	8	destruction	s	z
4	devise	s	z	9	use (n)	s	z
5	residence	s	z	10	use (v)	s	z

Test practice

Academic Reading

Questions 1–5

The reading passage has five sections, A–E.
Choose the correct heading for each section from the list of
headings below.
Write the correct number, i–viii, next to questions 1–5.

Test Tip
The headings in this type of question must
represent the ideas expressed throughout
each section, not just in one sentence.

> **List of headings**
>
> | i | Outdoor spaces in the house of tomorrow |
> |---|---|
> | ii | The house of the future helps with the battle of the sexes |
> | iii | The compact home of tomorrow |
> | iv | The multipurpose home of tomorrow |
> | v | Housework declines in the house of the future |
> | vi | Mixed success for visions of the future |
> | vii | The future lies in the past |
> | viii | A change of structure in the home of tomorrow |

1   Section A ....

2   Section B ....

3   Section C ....

4   Section D ....

5   Section E ....

The house of the future, then and now.

A

The term 'home of tomorrow' first came into usage in the 1920s to describe the 'ideal house for future living'
(Corn and Horrigan, 1984, p. 62). It quickly emerged as a cultural symbol for the American obsession with
the single-family dwelling. In the 1930s and 1940s, advertisers and promoters picked up the concept, and a
number of full-scale homes of tomorrow traveled through fairs and department stores. It was in this same era
that American consumer culture was consolidated. In the 1920s, there were three competing conceptions
of the home of the future. The first, indebted to modernist architecture, depicted the home of tomorrow as a
futuristic architectural structure. The second conception was that of the mass-produced, prefabricated house, a
dwelling potentially available to every North American. These first two failed to capture the imagination and the
dollars of industrialists or of the public, but the third image of the home of the future did. From World War II until
the present, the evolving story of the home of the future is a story of 'the house as a wonderland of gadgets'
(Horrigan, 1986, p.154).

B

In the 1950s, the home of the future was represented in and by one room: the kitchen. Appliance manufacturers,
advertisers and women's magazines teamed up to surround women with images of the technology of tomorrow
that would 'automate' their lives, and automation became a synonym for reduced domestic labor. In 1958, one
author predicted 'Combustion freezers and electric ovens may someday reduce the job of preparing meals to

a push-button operation' (Ross, 1958, pp.197–8). 'Before long there will also be self-propelled carpet and floor sweepers, automatic ironers that can fold and stack clothing, laundro-matic units that will wash and dry clothes even as these hang in the closet, dishwashers capable of washing and drying dinnerware and storing it in the cupboard, and many additional push-button marvels.' (Ross, 1958, p. 200)

The postwar faith in and fascination with science is very apparent in future predictions made in the 1950s. The magazine *Popular Mechanics* did a special feature in February 1950 entitled, 'Miracles You'll See in the Next Fifty Years'. 'Housewives in 50 years may wash dirty dishes – right down the drain! Cheap plastic would melt in hot water.' They also predicted that the housewife of the future would clean her house by simply turning the hose on everything. Furnishings, rugs, draperies and unscratchable floors would all be made of synthetic fabric or waterproof plastic. After the water had run down a drain in the middle of the floor (later concealed by a rug of synthetic fibre) you would turn on a blast of hot air and dry everything.

The overriding message of the 1950s vision of the house of the future is that one can access the wonders of the future through the purchase of domestic technology today. In an October 1957 issue of *Life* magazine, the built-in appliances from Westinghouse reflect the 'shape of tomorrow'. 'Put them in your home – suddenly you're living in the future.' As Corn and Horrigan (1984) noted, 'by focusing on improving technology ... the future becomes strictly a matter of things, their invention, improvement, and acquisition' (p. 11).

C

What is most striking in the 1960s home of the future is the recognition and incorporation of social and political turmoil into the representation of domestic technology. Technology moves out of the kitchen and spreads to the living room, bedroom and bathroom. While the home of the future was still a wonderland of gadgets, who was using the gadgets, why, and to what effect, was finally being opened up to possible alternatives. Whirlpool dishwashers ran an advertisement in November 1968 in *Ladies' Home Journal* explaining, 'How Whirlpool made my husband a man again'. Readers learned of the crisis of masculinity that can take place if a man helps with the housework. We learn that Barry is a great son, father and husband. He believed that the scrubbing of pots and pans was man's work and so he helped out at home. However, at work the men that work for him used to laugh behind his back because his hands were rough and red. The Whirlpool two-speed dishwasher stopped all that. Thus, a household appliance can preserve a man's masculinity by ensuring that he does not have to do 'women's work' in the home.

D

The broader social context continued to be reflected in the 1970s home of the future, but now the trend was to look backwards for the future, back to a proud pioneer heritage. In stark contrast to the 1950s, 'old-fashioned' is no longer used in a pejorative way; it is seen as a cherished value. Over the 1970s, North America experienced a certain erosion of trust in science and technology and there was less utopian speculation about the technologically produced future. The previous unproblematic link between technology, the future and progress was being questioned (Corn, 1986).

From the space-age metals of the 1960s where every object had an electrical cord, we find a return to the traditional. Ideal homes featured wood, inside and out, and an increased emphasis on windows. Domestic technologies were not featured as prominently, and the modernist or ultra-modernist designs of a few years earlier were all but gone. The use of wood, combined with the use of windows, worked to blur the line between outside and inside, bringing the outside into inner or domestic space.

We also see the influence of the Green movement, such as in the deployment of technology for solar-heated homes. The energy crisis was making itself felt, reflecting fears about a future not quite as rosy as that predicted by *Popular Mechanics* in 1950. Whereas in the 1960s the General Electric Company was exhorting consumers to 'Live Electrically', in the 1970s, the Edison Electric Company found it necessary to address the energy crisis directly in their advertisements.

E

In 1978, *House Beautiful* magazine, predicting what the homes of the 1980s would be like, suggested that self-indulgence was the wave of the future. 'Our senses are awakened, and a new technology is waiting to aid us in giving them a free rein. Bathroom spas and gyms, computerized kitchens, wide screen entertainment, even home discotheques are all on the way.' By the 1980s, the environmental and social movements of the 1970s were starting to ebb, significantly more women were working outside of the home, and computer technology was becoming more of a reality in the household. All these trends opened the door for a renewed love of technology.

The line between work and leisure became blurred in the 1980s. Forget about not being able to fit exercise into a hectic workday, in 1982, you can work and work out simultaneously. The Walking Desk, a computer workstation for the office at home, has a treadmill, stationary bike and stair climber installed underneath. On her most productive day, a worker should be able to walk four to five miles and burn as many as fifteen hundred calories while maintaining a normal workload. The desk will also come with a compact-disc player and color monitor for viewing nature scenes on a computer break. Thus, in addition to turning exercise into work, we see that nature is being brought into the home for breaks. One never has to leave the home, but the imperative is still clearly to be productive.

Questions 6–13

Look at the following list of statements (questions 6–13).
Match each statement or prediction with the correct time period, A–E.
Write the correct letter, A–E, next to questions 6–13.
NB You may use any letter more than once.

6   There was a loss of faith in automation. ....

7   Advertisers believed that houses would be made in a factory. ....

8   There were fewer housewives. ....

9   One writer envisaged furniture being made from fully washable materials. ....

10   There was an increased awareness of the environment. ....

11   There was a link between our interest in the future and increased consumerism. ....

12   One magazine predicted that disposable plates would be used. ....

13   A new expression for 'the perfect home' was introduced. ....

List of time periods
A   1920s
B   1930s and 1940s
C   1950s
D   1970s
E   1980s

---

12 Information technology

Telecommunications, computers and technology

Telecommunications

1.1 Before you listen, answer these questions.

One of the first mobile phones

1 Do you have: a mobile phone; a laptop computer; a portable music device; an email address?

2 How long have you had it/them?

3 If you need to connect to the Internet, what do you use? How long does it take you?

4 How would you describe the technology you use?
A   up-to-date   B   dated   C   state-of-the-art

5 How do you prefer to stay in touch with people?
A   by post   B   by email   C   by phone

1.2 🎧 12a Listen to a conversation about two different mobile phones and say whether the questions below apply to

A   the Smart Phone

B   the Optima

C   both the Smart Phone and the Optima.

Which phone

1 is <u>small</u>? ..(A) compact...............

2 is <u>easy to use</u>? ....

3 has <u>normal phone buttons</u>? ....

4 <u>shows</u> a calendar <u>without being asked</u>?
   ....

5 has <u>the most up-to-date</u> technology?
   ....

6 can <u>obtain information from the Internet</u>?
   ....

1.3 🎧 12a Now listen again and next to your answers in **1.2** write the words that paraphrase the underlined words.

1.4 Complete the crossword with words from the recording.

Across

1   easy to use

3   open a computer file

6   move up or down on a screen

7   work a machine

9   the keys on a computer, typewriter or piano

11 an action or purpose something is designed for

Down

2   show on a screen

4   have specific tools

5   save or keep safe

8   the part of a computer that stores information

10 information

1.5 (🎧 12b) Listen to five people speaking. Each one has forgotten the name for something. What is the word they need to use?

Speaker A: I use my .... every day.
Speaker B: I use my computer as a ....
Speaker C: I would like to get a ....
Speaker D: I can't imagine what it was like without ....
Speaker E: I would love to get my mother a ....
Which two of the words you have used needed the suffix *-or*?

Computers and technology

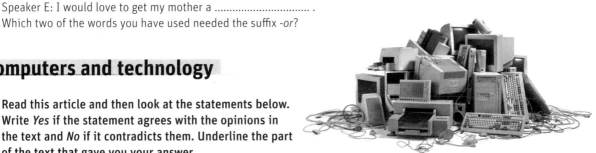

2.1 Read this article and then look at the statements below. Write *Yes* if the statement agrees with the opinions in the text and *No* if it contradicts them. Underline the part of the text that gave you your answer.

Has the present lived up to the expectations of the past? Throughout the ages people have tried to predict what life in the twenty-first century would be like. Many science-fiction writers did manage to predict the influence the computer would have on our world. Some even imagined that it would take over our lives, develop a personality, and turn on its creators. To some extent they were right, especially when it comes to children and **cyber** addiction. One constant prediction was that, thanks to computers and machines, the time devoted to labour would diminish. Even in 1971, in his book Future Shock, Alvin Toffler envisaged a society awash with 'free time'. The author noted that time at work had been cut in half since the turn of the previous century and wrongly **speculated** that it would be cut in half again by 2000.

However, our **gadget**-filled homes are a tribute to the various visions of the future: the microwave oven, internet fridges with ice-cube dispensers, freezers, video **monitors**, climate control, dishwashers, washing machines, personal computers, wireless connections and cupboards full of instant food. These may no longer be considered **cutting-edge** but they have matched, if not **surpassed**, visions of how we would live. The domestic robot never quite happened, but if you can phone ahead to set the heating and use a remote control to operate the garage door, they may as well be redundant.

The car, of course, has failed to live up to our expectations. It has been given turbo engines, DVD players and automatic windows, but its tyres stick stubbornly to the road. Why doesn't it take off? The past promised us a flying car in various guises. In 1947 a **prototype** circled San Diego for more than an hour but later crashed in the desert. Some 30 patents for flying cars were registered in the US patent office last century but none of these ideas has been transformed into a commercially available vehicle.

At least communication technology in this **digital** age hasn't let us down. Even in the most remote areas people have access to some form of communication **device**. The introduction of the telephone last century changed our world, but today's mobile phones and the **virtual** world of the Internet have revolutionised it.

1   A modern problem proves that computers are dominating our lives in some way. ....Yes....
2   Alan Toffler's predictions have been proven true. ....
3   Household gadgets today have been a disappointment. ....
4   We have enough gadgets now to make robots unnecessary in the home. ....
5   Today's cars have fulfilled all predictions. ....
6   The mobile phone and the Internet have changed our world for the better. ....

2.2 Now match the words in bold in the text with these definitions.

1 guessed ....

2 a machine invented for a specific purpose (× 2)
....

3 the first working example of a machine
....

4 almost real ....

5 very modern ....

6 be greater than expected ....

7 relating to computers ....

8 a screen that images can be seen on
....

9 an adjective used to describe anything related to computers ....

2.3 COMPOUND WORDS Match a word from box A with a word from box B and use the compound words to complete the sentences below.

| A | automatic | cyber | labour | remote |
| | silicon | wireless | | |

| B | chip | connection | control | pilot |
| | saving | space | | |

1 I can access the Internet from anywhere in my house because my laptop has a ....

2 The invention of the .... made watching television an even more passive experience.

3 In my view the dishwasher is one of the greatest .... devices.

4 People often talk about emails and text messages being lost in .... as if it were a real place.

5 Even flying a plane has been automated now. The .... is used for most of the flight.

6 The invention of the .... meant that computers could be much smaller.

2.4 Correct the mistakes in the text. Use ONE WORD only. Hyphenated words (e.g. *state-of-the-art*) count as one word.

Today's ¹*advance* technology has brought many benefits. For example, nowadays we have many ²*small tools* that can save time in the home and, if you have access ³*with* a computer and a telephone ⁴*connect* then you can work almost anywhere you choose. What is more, modern software ⁵*programmes* are so user-friendly that you don't even need a great deal of computer knowledge to be able to ⁶*play* them.

However, there are some disadvantages to the ⁷*technology* era. For example, people today want to have the very ⁸*last* technology but, as new technology dates very quickly, an increasing amount of computer hardware is being dumped. This adds to our already serious pollution problems. Furthermore, ⁹*computerise* has led to fewer jobs and less human contact as many everyday transactions are now done ¹⁰*with* computer rather than manually.

1 .... *advanced* ....

2 ....

3 ....

4 ....

5 ....

6 ....

7 ....

8 ....

9 ....

10 ....

> **Error warning!**
>
> Note the following spellings of the word *program*: computer **program** (UK and US spelling), television **programme** (UK spelling only). Note the different forms of *computer*: *computerise* (verb); *computerisation* (noun); *computerised* (adj): *We use a computerised system.* NOT *a computerise system.* Automated can be used in a similar way, but includes machines as well as computers: *Our processing system is fully automated.* We talk about *the computer era, the digital era* or *the technological era.* NOT *the technology era.*

Test practice

Speaking Test

Part 1 (4–5 minutes)

1 Can you tell me about your hometown?

2 What kind of things do you do on a typical day?

3 What form of transport do you usually use?

4 What kind of things do you enjoy doing with your friends?

5 What did you do last weekend?

6 What are your plans for after this test?

Part 2 (3–4 minutes)

In this part of the test you are going to talk about a topic for about 2 minutes. Here is a card with some questions on it. You have about one minute to prepare and you can make notes if you wish.

> Describe something you have bought recently.
> You should say
> - what you bought
> - what it looks like
> - why you bought it
> and say whether you are pleased with your purchase.

Part 3 (4–5 minutes)

1 If you could buy any new gadget you wanted, what would you choose and why?

2 Do you think people today spend too much money buying new things? (Why?)

3 Do you always want to buy the latest technology or are you happy with an older model? (Why?)

4 Why do you think older people struggle so much with new technology?

5 Are there any ways we could help them to adapt?

6 What changes in technology do you think we will see in the next 50 years?

7 Do you think we should always try to improve on existing technology or are some things better as they are? (Why?)

13 The modern world
Globalisation, changing attitudes and trends

Globalisation

1.1 Answer these questions.

1 How many of the following brand names do you know?
   Nike   Sony   Coca Cola   Levi's   Versace   Gucci   Adidas

2 Can you name the countries these companies are from?

3 Can you name a product or brand from your country that is well known in other countries?

1.2 (🎧 13a) Listen to two people, Amy and Bill, discussing globalisation. Who expresses the following opinions? Write A for Amy and B for Bill.

1 Globalisation could harm the regional **way of life**. ....

2 Globalisation can help people who live **within a small area**. ....

3 **Worldwide**, more people eat traditional food than fast food. ....

4 People can enjoy products **from many different cultures** today. ....

5 **Large overseas companies have control over** the non-alcoholic drink market. ....

6 If not for globalisation, companies from different countries would not **join together** to do business. ....

7 People who travel prefer to see **unusual and exciting** things instead of **symbols** used by big companies. ....

8 Experiencing something from another country does not take away your **feeling of belonging to your country**. ....

9 **A range of different cultures** can be reflected in food bought overseas. ....

10 No single company **has complete control over** the fashion industry. ....

1.3 (🎧 13a) Now listen again and write the words or phrases from the conversation that mean the same as the words in bold in **1.2**.

way of life = culture; ....

....

1.4 WORD BUILDING
Complete the table.

Noun	Adjective
culture	
	ethnic
globalisation	
	modern
	multicultural
nation	
	urban

Changing attitudes and trends

2.1 Read the article and then look at the statements below. Write *Yes* if the statement agrees with the opinions in the text and *No* if it contradicts them. Underline the part of the text that gave you your answer.

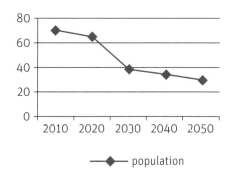

population

The past 40 years have seen astounding developments: globalisation, the end of the Cold War, the Internet. The next 40 years may bring even more profound changes. In order to predict the future we must first examine the past. Historians see history as being driven by a combination of cumulative long-term trends and short to mid-term <u>cycles, each of which contains the seeds of a subsequent but familiar situation</u>. There have been many projections about the future which, with the benefit of hindsight, seem rather ridiculous. Who can forget the predictions about the Y2K bug when commentators believed that societies would collapse and satellites would fall from the sky? Unfortunately, as a result, many people today are more sceptical about current predictions concerning global warming.

One of the few areas in which long-term trends can be clearly seen is demographic statistics. These indicate that the population of the world will increase to about eight billion in 2026 and continue to rise to nine billion by 2050, after which it will flatten out. Some societies have birth rates that are already locking their populations into absolute decline. Not only will the populations of each of these societies dwindle, but an increasing proportion will be moving into old age, when they are less productive and use more health resources. However, the weakness of all such predictions is that humans meddle with their own history. Predictions about the future affect how humans act or plan today and ultimately how events unfold. The challenge is to pick the trends that are likely to be prolonged, but to also factor in human influence.

1 A cycle is usually repeated at some time **in the future**. <u>yes.</u>

2 We can **look back and understand** past predictions. ....

3 Past predictions have caused people to **firmly believe in** current predictions. ....

4 **Population figures** can be predicted quite accurately. ....

5 Some **countries** are predicted to experience a **total** decline in population. ....

6 The **percentage** of elderly people will **dwindle** in some countries. ....

7 Elderly people **work less**. ....

8 To make accurate predictions we need to **take into account** the **effect** people have on their environment. ....

2.2 Look at the words in bold in the eight statements and find the words or phrases in the text that are similar in meaning, or the opposite. The first one has been done for you.

1 <u>in the future – subsequent</u>

2 ....

3 ....

4 ....

5 (×2).. ....

6 (×2) ....

7 ....

8 (×2) ....

Error warning!

Per cent is the word form of the symbol %. We can write *20%* or *20 per cent*. *Percentage* is the noun form: *The **percentage** of women in Parliament increased in 2001.* NOT ~~The percent of women~~ ...

2.3 Correct the six mistakes in the text. Use the information in unit **23** to help you.

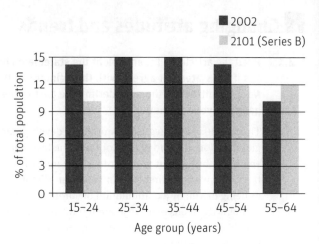

2002
2101 (Series B)

The graph displays the actual population of Australia in 2002 and the projected figures of 2101. The per cent of people aged 15–24 is predicted to fall significantly during this period, while there will be an increase of the percentage of people aged 55–64. In 2002, just under 15 percentage of the population was aged between 15 and 24, while in 2101 this is predicted to drop in approximately 10 per cent.

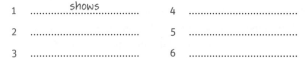

1 ....shows........   4 ....

2 ....   5 ....

3 ....   6 ....

2.4 Complete the text with suitable words from the box.

ageing   challenges   compounded   declining   elderly   factors   implications   migrating
population   present   rates   trends

Statistics show that in many countries the population will decline in the next 50 years. The population of these countries will also age rapidly. What effect will this have on those countries?
If current (1).............................. continue, then in some countries the (2).............................. is expected to dwindle within the next 50 years. This problem is (3).............................. by the fact that not only is the number of inhabitants diminishing, but they are also growing older. This (4).............................. population will bring its own (5).............................. . At (6).............................. there are sufficient younger people to earn money and pay taxes to support the (7).............................. . However, within 50 years this will not be the case. There are several possible (8).............................. contributing to this problem. First, birth (9).............................. in these countries are clearly falling. Second, there could be an increase in the number of people (10).............................. away from these areas. The ageing and (11).............................. population is expected to have important (12).............................. for the labour force and the quality of everyday life.

3.1 PRONUNCIATION Which of the patterns (A–F) matches the number of syllables and the stress pattern of the words below? (For example, pattern A matches the word *global* because it has two syllables with a stress on the first syllable.)

A   B   C   D   E   F
•   •   •   •   •   •
_ _   _ _ _   _ _ _ _   _ _ _   _ _ _ _   _ _ _ _

global ..A...   culture ....   sceptical ....   projection ....
globalisation ....   domestic ....   modernisation ....
implication ....   international ....   national ....
isolation ....   local ....   multicultural ....

3.2 🎧 13b Now listen and check your answers, then practise saying the words.

Test practice

Academic Writing Task 1

Test Tip

Don't copy information from the question paper, use your own words. Make sure that you describe the most important information and that your figures are accurate. Check your spelling when you have finished and make sure you have written at least 150 words. Study the information in unit 23 before you begin.

You should spend about 20 minutes on this task.

The graph below shows the average growth in domestic products in wealthy countries, countries that have adopted a global approach to business and countries that have not.

Write a report for a university lecturer describing the information below.

Write at least 150 words.

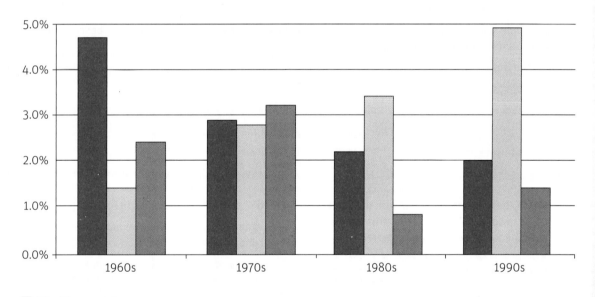

Average annual Gross Domestic Product (GDP) growth

■ Wealthy countries
□ Globalisers
■ Non-globalisers

Key
Globalisers = developing countries adopting a global approach to business.
Non-globalisers = developing countries adopting a non-global approach to business.

14 Urbanisation
Problems and solutions, big city life

Problems and solutions

1.1 Consider whether you can ever have *too much*, *too many*, *too little* or *too few* of the following.

time   traffic   people   money   space   work   rubbish

1.2 🔊 14a Listen to a conversation between two women and decide which two topics they talk about.

1.3 🔊 14a Listen again and write down all the verbs that are used with the words *problem* and *issue*.

....
....
....
....

1.4 Complete the sentences using the verbs you wrote in **1.3**. There may be more than one possible answer, so try to use a different verb for each sentence.

1   One of the biggest problems .... the world today is poverty.

2   Your problems won't go away if you ignore them, you need to .... them.

3   The problem was .... by a blocked pipe, which eventually burst.

4   Here is a list of the issues that will be .... during the meeting.

5   Unfortunately we were unable to .... the issue, even after two days of talks.

6   The main speaker did not arrive, which .... an awkward problem for the organisers of the conference.

1.5 Match the nouns in column B with the correct verbs in column A. Which two verbs can be used with the words *problem* and *compromise*?

A	B
find	a compromise
overcome	an issue
solve	a situation
remedy	a difficulty
resolve	a solution
reach	a problem

1.6 Correct the mistakes in these sentences.

1   I am not sure we will ever ~~solve the issue~~ of unemployment.

2   We need to resolve a solution to this situation as soon as possible.

3   What can we do to solve this difficulty?

4   At last scientists have solution the problems associated with solar-powered cars.

5   Finally, the members of the city council were able to solve a compromise and the building work was allowed to start.

1   solve the problem / resolve the issue
    ....

2   4   ....

3   5   ....

1.7 Cross out the one word in each list that is NOT a synonym for the word in capitals.

1 PROBLEM   difficulty, dilemma, ~~benefit~~, challenge, obstacle

2 SOLUTION   answer, key, remedy, resolution, setback

3 WORSEN   compound, deteriorate, enhance, exacerbate

4 IMPROVE   advance, aggravate, flourish, progress, reform

5 CHANGE   acclimatise, adapt, adjust, amend, linger, modify, transform

> ### Vocabulary note
> We usually use a hyphen between two words if they are joined together to form an adjective: *user-friendly*. We don't use a hyphen if the first word ends in *-ly*: *environmentally friendly*

1.8 Use a hyphen to combine one of the words in box A with one of the words in box B. Then complete the sentences.

| A | double | long | short | one | B | edged | sighted | sided | term |

1 We need a .... plan for our transport systems that will take into account future growth.

2 A warning sign was put at the site of the accident as a .... measure until a new wall was built.

3 This argument appears to be a little .... I'd like to hear the other side as well.

4 The management agreed to employ five more members of staff, which in hindsight was a very ....
   decision because within a few weeks we were still understaffed.

5 Globalisation is a .... sword. It promotes multiculturalism while it erodes the local culture.

Big city life

2.1 Complete the text with suitable adjectives from the box. More than one adjective may be possible.

adequate   basic   booming   catastrophic   decent
enormous   pressing   staggering

Megacities

The world's population is [1]..............................., no more so than in its cities. Today, there are 21 megacities, each containing more than 10 million inhabitants, three-quarters of them in developing nations. By 2020, there are expected to be at least 27 megacities. Such a [2]............................... rate of urbanisation brings its own problems, especially in developing nations, where the majority of the megacities will be found.

Employment and educational opportunities are the main attraction of urban centres. But hopes for a better life are often dashed as overpopulation puts an [3]............................... strain on the infrastructure of the cities and their ability to provide [4]............................... necessities such as clean water and a place to live.

Many rural migrants fail to find [5]............................... work, and therefore cannot afford [6]...............................
housing. In some megacities up to 50 per cent of the residents live in slums. This problem is
[7]..............................., with the United Nations predicting that half the world's population will be living in cities by next year. If the infrastructure within those cities does not grow at the same rate the result will be
[8]............................... .

2.2 Find words in the text on page 73 that match these definitions.

1 People that live in a particular place. ....

2 Areas of the world that are poorer and have less advanced industries. ....

3 The process by which more people leave the countryside to live in the city. ....

4 The problem of having too many people. ....

5 The basic systems and services of a city. ....

6 Very poor and crowded areas of a city. ....

2.3 WORD BUILDING Complete the table.

Noun	Verb	Adjective
competition		
		excluded
	include	
	isolate	
		poor
responsibility	.... responsibility	
		tolerant

3.1 Answer these questions. Write one or two sentences.

1 What are the main problems associated with living in a big city?

2 Can anything be done to solve those problems?

3 Whose responsibility is it to solve these problems?

> **V** Vocabulary note
>
> To refer to a group of people we can use *the* + adjective: *the elderly, the poor, the young.* E.g. *We should look after **the elderly**.*

3.2 Now complete these answers to the questions with suitable words from **2.3**.

1 Big cities can be overcrowded, so there are a lot of people c............................... for each job and for accommodation. The lack of jobs usually means that there is a lot of p............................... in big cities. And although there are a lot of people around you, many people feel very i............................... in big cities and it's particularly difficult for the elderly.

2 I think we need to be more t............................... of each other. I think it helps if we try to create small communities within the bigger city so we should try to i............................... people rather than e............................... them.

3 Well, we all have to t............................... r............................... for these problems and we can all do something to help. But the government is also r............................... to a certain extent as well. They need to make sure that the p............................... are looked after and that they have access to the facilities they need.

4 PRONUNCIATION 🔊 14b If we have *-ed* at the end of a word, it can be pronounced with a *t* or *d* sound. Look at the following words and write *t* or *d* depending on their sound. Now listen and check your answers, then practise saying the words.

> accepted   crowded   developed   excluded   included   isolated
> overpriced   overworked   resolved   stressed   solved

Test practice

Academic Reading

Rags, bones and recycling bins

Tim Cooper investigates the history of waste recovery.

As concern mounts that the consumer society may be ecologically unsustainable, historians have begun to interest themselves in past efforts to achieve efficient use of scarce resources. Far from being a recent innovation, recycling and reuse of household cast-offs have a long history. In early modern Britain, one of the most characteristic forms of recycling has been the trade in second-hand clothing, which has survived to the present day in the shape of the ubiquitous charity shop. The cost of buying new ensured that many among the lower orders of eighteenth-century English society relied on second-hand apparel. The rag fairs of the rapidly growing cities and a network of tradesmen and pawnbrokers supplied this trade. Some historians have argued that the second-hand trade played an important role in the nascent development of mass consumerism and fashion; demand was so high that there was a ready market for stolen clothes.

Recycling was not restricted to the clothing trade. A much wider culture of reuse existed. This included, for example, the recycling of building materials from demolished buildings, the repair or reuse of most metal goods, and the use of old rags in the paper industry. The paper industry was almost wholly reliant upon recycling for its raw materials. Recycling was thus an important component of the pre-industrial economy, enabling it to cope with shortages of raw materials and aiding the poor. Pre-industrial recycling was largely a response to chronically low levels of production. After 1800, industrialisation, urbanisation and population growth would see the emergence of a new problem – waste – and give a new significance to recycling.

Of course, the generation of urban waste was not new in itself, but the scale of waste production after 1800 certainly was. The treatment and disposal of domestic waste became a problem of the first order. From the 1850s the problem of human waste disposal was being addressed by the construction of sewerage systems; the domestic refuse problem, however, remained relatively neglected until 1875. Up until 1900 most urban areas relied on private contractors for waste disposal, who operated only with the minimum of environmental regulation. This was the context in which the Victorian dust-yards, immortalised in Charles Dickens' novel *Our Mutual Friend*, emerged.

These yards sprang up either in or around many major cities in the nineteenth century, but were particularly characteristic of London. The dust-yards made their money by employing men, women and children to sift and sort through the filth in search of items of value, such as rags and metals. These were then sold to contract merchants. A large proportion of the material that remained after sorting was dust and cinders; where possible these were sold as a fertiliser or fuel source, but where no market existed they were dumped either on land or at sea.

The dust-yards were the most notorious of the nineteenth-century waste trades. In *Dangerous Trade* (1902), industrial health expert Thomas Oliver stated that 'under all circumstances dust-sorting is dirty and disagreeable work'. The uniquely unpleasant conditions of the yards meant that dust-women formed 'a class by themselves, and so the work becomes more or less hereditary'. The workers also received marginal reward for their efforts. By 1900 the average wages of women in contractors' yards in London were only between seven and eight shillings per week. As a result the dust-yards were increasingly controversial by the end of the nineteenth century. At the same time, the waste continued to grow. The 1875 Public Health Act had given local authorities a legal responsibility to remove and dispose of domestic waste. However, the last years of the century saw a solution to the apparently insoluble problem of what to do with the refuse of Britain's cities. A means, in the eyes of experts, to achieve the perfect removal of waste without resort to either the dust-yard or the tip: the incinerator.

Test Tip

For notes completion items, make sure that you stick to the word limit. Do not write extra unnecessary words. Check you have copied the words correctly from the text.

Questions 1–7

Complete the notes using **NO MORE THAN TWO WORDS** from the text.

The history of recycling in the UK

Eighteenth-century Britain

- People recycled products such as
  – used (1) ....
  – (2) ....
  – anything made from (3) ....
  – old cloth.

- The (4) .... business relied heavily on recycled materials.

- Recycling had two main advantages:
  – it provided necessary (5) ....
  – it helped (6) ....

Nineteenth-century Britain

- More refuse was created by an increase in the number of
  i)   big cities
  ii) inhabitants
  and
  iii) increasing (7) ....

Questions 8–13

Complete the flowchart below using **NO MORE THAN TWO WORDS** from the text.

The processing of waste up until the 1900s

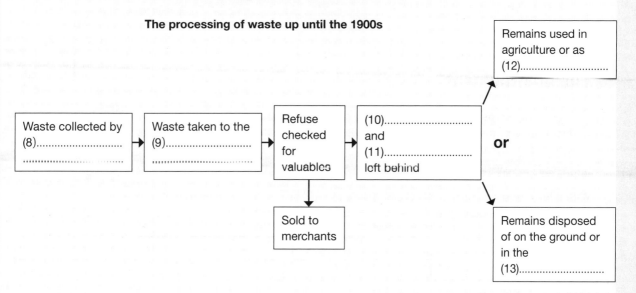

Question 14

Choose the correct answer **A**, **B**, **C** or **D**.

In the final paragraph, what are we told about waste disposal at the end of the nineteenth century?
A   It was a respected business.
B   The work was relatively well-paid.
C   Authorities decided to burn the waste.
D   Disposal of waste had not yet been regulated.

15 The green revolution
The environment, climate change and pollution

The environment

1.1 Choose the words that reflect your opinion of these three statements from the first column of the table below. Write the words you chose in the *My Opinion* column.

1 We should educate the public about our environment by handing out leaflets.

2 Within a few years we will have solved all of our pollution problems.

3 Within the next ten years the only chemicals we use will be environmentally friendly ones.

	My opinion	*Speaker A*	*Speaker B*
Statement 1–useful / useless?			
Statement 2–possible / impossible?			
Statement 3–likely / unlikely?			

1.2 (🎧 15a) Now listen to two people (speakers A and B) giving their opinions about the same ideas and choose the words that reflect their opinions. Write them in the appropriate columns of the table.

1.3 Listen again or look at the recording script at the back of the book and write the adjectives the speakers used to express their opinions. Put the adjectives into the correct column according to their meaning.

useful	useless	possible	impossible	likely	unlikely
beneficial	....	....	....	....	....
....	....	....	....	....	....
....	....	....	....	....	....
....	....	....	....	....	....

> **(V) Vocabulary note**
>
> The prefix *re-* often tells us that something is being done again: *reuse, revegetate*.
> The prefix *de-* often tells us that something is being removed: *decaffeinated, deforestation*.

Climate change and pollution

2.1 Complete the text with words from the box.

> acid   biodiversity   contaminated   deforestation   ecosystems   emissions
> environmental   erosion   exhaust   drought   fertilisers   greenhouse   waste

The advances made by humans have made us the dominant species on our planet. However, several eminent scientists are concerned that we have become too successful, that our way of life is putting an **unprecedented** strain on the Earth's (1)............................... and threatening our future as a species. We are confronting (2)............................... problems that are more **taxing** than ever before, some of them seemingly **insoluble**. Many of the Earth's crises are **chronic** and **inexorably** linked. Pollution is an obvious example of this affecting our air, water and soil.

The air is polluted by (3)............................... produced by cars and industry. Through (4)............................... rain and (5)............................... gases these same (6)............................... fumes can have a **devastating** impact on our climate. Climate change is arguably the greatest environmental challenge facing our planet with increased storms, floods, (7)............................... and species losses predicted. This will **inevitably** have a negative impact on (8)............................... and thus our ecosystem.

The soil is (9)............................... by factories and power stations which can leave heavy metals in the soil. Other human activities such as the overdevelopment of land and the clearing of trees also take their toll on the quality of our soil; (10)............................... has been shown to cause soil (11)............................... . Certain farming practices can also pollute the land though the use of chemical pesticides and (12)............................... . This contamination in turn affects our rivers and waterways and damages life there. The chemicals enter our food chain, moving from fish to mammals to us. Our crops are also grown on land that is far from **pristine**. Affected species include the polar bear, so not even the Arctic is **immune**.

Reducing (13)............................... and clearing up pollution costs money. Yet it is our quest for wealth that generates so much of the refuse. There is an urgent need to find a way of life that is less damaging to the Earth. This is not easy, but it is **vital**, because pollution is **pervasive** and often life-threatening.

2.2 **Match the words in bold with these synonyms.**

1 unspoiled ....*pristine*...........

2 crucial ....

3 unparalleled ....

4 extremely harmful ....

5 insurmountable ....

6 unaffected ....

7 omnipresent ....

8 unavoidably (×2) ....

9 persistent ....

10 challenging ....

3 **Consider how you would answer these questions.**

1 What do you think is the greatest environmental threat we face today?

2 What can the government do to help protect the environment?

3 What can we as individuals do?

4.1 Use a dictionary to check the different forms of the words in the box as well as the prepositions used with them. Then complete the answers to the questions in **3** using the correct form of the word in brackets. You will need to add prepositions to the words that are underlined.

contaminate   danger   dispose   erode   pollute   recycle   risk   sustain   threat

1 I think our environment is [1] *under threat from* (*threat*) many different things. We have allowed too much [2]............................... (*pollute*) to enter our ecosystem and we are [3]............................... (*danger*) poisoning ourselves as a result. I think soil [4]............................... (*erode*) and water [5]............................... (*contaminate*) are two of the most urgent problems that we need to deal with.

2 Clearly our current lifestyle is not [6]............................... (*sustain*). The government should educate people about these problems and encourage us to change our habits. They need to show everyone that we are putting the very future of our planet [7]............................... (*risk*).

3 We can make sure we don't throw [8]............................... (*recycle*) items into our normal waste [9]............................... (*dispose*) bins. We can also help protect our planet by not using phosphate-based detergents; this will help to keep [10]............................... (*pollute*) out of our food chain.

4.2 Complete the sentences using the negative form of the words in brackets.

1   It is .... *unrealistic* .... (*realistic*) to expect everyone to change their buying habits overnight.

2   When it comes to protecting the environment, cost should be .... (*relevant*).

3   It is .... (*reasonable*) for rich countries to expect developing countries to reduce carbon emissions immediately.

4   People who dump chemical waste into our waterways are very .... (*responsible*) .

5   The oil spill has caused .... (*repairable*) damage to several marine species.

6   Scientists believe that the damage to this area is .... (*reversible*) .

7   These species are ....(*replaceable*) . Once they are lost our ecosystem will be changed.

8   It is a mistake to think that increased consumerism and environmental damage are .... (*related*) .

 Vocabulary note

The prefix *ir-* is often used with adjectives beginning with *r* to form the opposite or to mean lacking something: *reversible*, ***ir**reversible*, *regular*, ***ir**regular*. Some words beginning with *r* form their opposite with *un-*: *realistic*, *unrealistic*.

5   PRONUNCIATION 🎧 15b Some words have a different stress pattern and therefore a different pronunciation, depending on their meaning or part of speech. Circle the correct stress pattern for the words in *italics* in these sentences. Listen to the recording to check your answers and then practise saying the sentences.

1   I *refuse* to go. (r**e**fuse / ref**u**se)

2   Disposing of *refuse* is a growing problem. (r**e**fuse / ref**u**se)

3   There is a *conflict* here. (c**o**nflict / confl**i**ct)

4   The two reports *conflict* each other. (c**o**nflict / confl**i**ct)

5   We all need to be *present* at the meeting. (pr**e**sent / pres**e**nt)

6   This issue *presents* an enormous problem. (pr**e**sents / pres**e**nts)

7   We are making a lot of *progress*. (pr**o**gress / progr**e**ss)

8   We need to *progress* at a faster rate. (pr**o**gress / progr**e**ss)

9   There has been an *increase* in carbon emissions. (**in**crease / incr**ea**se)

10   Temperatures are expected to *increase*. (**in**crease / incr**ea**se)

Test practice

Academic Writing Task 1

Test Tip

Make sure that you include all of the stages in the process. You should follow
a logical sequence and do not miss any stages out. Do not copy words directly
from the question paper, instead try to change them. For example, you could
use the verb *collect* instead of the noun *collection*. Study the information in
unit 23 before you begin.

You should spend about 20 minutes on this task.

Write a report for a university lecturer describing the information below.

Write at least 150 words.

The flowchart below shows the recycling process of aluminium cans.

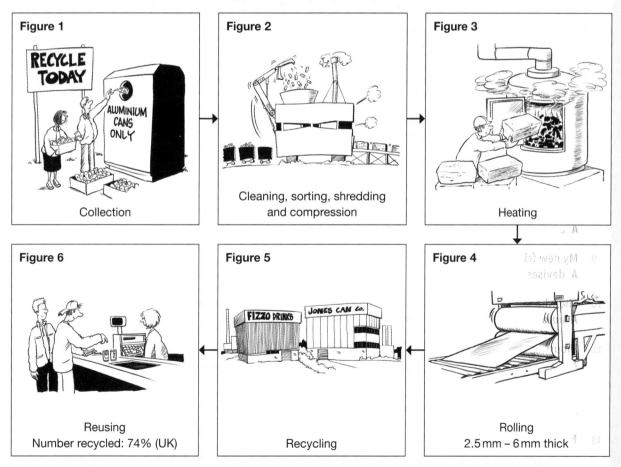

Figure 1	Figure 2	Figure 3
Collection	Cleaning, sorting, shredding and compression	Heating

Figure 6	Figure 5	Figure 4
Reusing Number recycled: 74% (UK)	Recycling	Rolling 2.5 mm – 6 mm thick

Choose the correct letter A, B, C or D.

1   The tallest building where I live has 75 ....
    A stores   **B** storages   **C** stories   **D** storeys

2   It is a very .... house, you can't really tell it apart from all the others in the street.
    A ornate   **B** innovative   **C** traditional   **D** state-of-the-art

3   I wish someone would invent a .... for opening milk cartons – my family always makes a mess of it!
    A devise   **B** device   **C** trigger   **D** pulley

4   Although it is an old house, it has been very well ....
    A maintained   **B** condemned   **C** occupied   **D** demolished

5   The latest .... for consumers is a system that allows shoppers to check out their groceries for themselves without having to wait in long queues.
    A innovate   **B** inventor   **C** innovator   **D** innovation

6   The developers .... a school on the new housing estate.
    A build   **B** building   **C** built   **D** built up

7   This machine performs the same .... as a washing machine but on a much larger scale.
    A function   **B** frame   **C** feature   **D** form

8   The Internet allows us to .... enormous amounts of information without leaving the house.
    A access   **B** accept   **C** scroll   **D** supply

9   My new fridge has a little screen on the outside that .... the internal and external temperature.
    A devises   **B** designs   **C** displays   **D** discovers

10   The whole system has been .... so we can no longer ask anyone for help.
    A automatic   **B** automated   **C** computerise   **D** digital

11   I found a very useful article .... the Internet.
    A by   **B** in   **C** for   **D** on

12   Our new house was designed .... computer.
    A by   **B** in   **C** on   **D** with

13   Many big cities today are ...., with inhabitants from all over the world.
    A culture   **B** cultural   **C** multiculture   **D** multicultural

14   International prices can also have an impact on the .... market.
    A domestic   **B** global   **C** urban   **D** worldwide

15 The graph shows the figures .... 2003 and 2005.
    A of   **B** to   **C** for   **D** about

16 The chart shows the .... of visitors and their country of origin.
    A per cent   **B** percentage   **C** %   **D** total

17 I think we all need to do more to help ....
    A old   **B** old person   **C** elderly   **D** the elderly

18 Our .... population will cause many problems in the future.
    A age   **B** ageing   **C** elderly   **D** old

19 We really need to find a way to .... this issue.
    A solve   **B** overcome   **C** prevent   **D** resolve

20 The bad weather and a lack of food simply .... our problems.
    A compounded   **B** enhanced   **C** salvaged   **D** transformed

21 Given the rapid growth of our population, there is a .... need to improve our infrastructure.
    A huge   **B** catastrophic   **C** pressing   **D** booming

22 If people were more .... of each other then there would be less fighting.
    A excluding   **B** exclusive   **C** tolerate   **D** tolerant

23 We all need to .... responsibility for improving our local community.
    A have   **B** make   **C** take   **D** give

24 After a few hours of discussion we finally reached a ....
    A compromise   **B** promise   **C** situation   **D** solution

25 Some scientists believe that we are in danger .... running out of oil within ten years.
    A from   **B** for   **C** of   **D** to

26 Many jobs are at .... if the current financial climate continues.
    A danger   **B** risk   **C** dangerous   **D** threat

27 Cleaning detergent is a common household .... that can be found in our waterways.
    A pollution   **B** pollutant   **C** polluter   **D** polluted

28 It is difficult to quantify the .... that household waste has on the environment.
    A affect   **B** effort   **C** impact   **D** implication

29 Every household should be more careful in the way that they .... of waste.
    A dispose   **B** disposal   **C** eliminate   **D** throw

30 The government have .... to fine anyone who pollutes the river.
    A endangered   **B** risked   **C** prevented   **D** threatened

16 The energy crisis
Natural resources, alternative fuels

Natural resources

1.1 Answer the questions in this quiz.

1   You decide to fly to an island 5,000 miles away for a holiday. How many trees would you need to plant to offset or make up for the CO_2 emissions produced by the flight?
    A   0.2   B   20   C   2

2   Which is the most environmentally friendly way to clean your clothes?
    A   Hand-wash the clothes in hot water.
    B   Take them to the dry cleaners.
    C   Machine-wash the clothes in cold water.

3   You are tidying up your house in the evening, going back and forth between the bedroom, kitchen and living room, spending five to ten minutes in each room as you sort out the clutter. What is the best way to make sure your lights aren't needlessly wasting energy?
    A   Keep the lights on as you go from room to room until the job is done.
    B   Turn the lights off every time you leave a room and then on again when you return.

4   You decide to cook a baked potato for lunch. Which is the most energy-efficient way of cooking the potato?
    A   Put it in an electric oven to cook slowly for an hour.
    B   Quickly zap it in the microwave.

5   You want to really make a significant contribution to the reduction of CO_2 emissions. Which of these would be of the most benefit over the course of a year?
    A   Taking the train instead of driving a car.
    B   Hanging your washing out to dry rather than using the tumble dryer.
    C   Working from home one day a week.

1.2 (16) Listen to the answers to find out how environmentally aware you are.

1.3 Complete the text with one word in each gap. Then look at the recording script at the back of the book to check your answers.

If we want to (1)......................... energy then we need to change the way we behave. We need to buy appliances that are more energy (2)......................... and limit the amount of time we use them. To reduce the (3)......................... the greenhouse gases have on our (4)......................... we should plant more trees. Trees can (5)......................... carbon dioxide and so they help to (6)......................... the fumes produced by our cars. Turning off lights even for a few minutes can (7)......................... the negative effects of turning them on again later.

2.1 Read the text and then answer the questions below.

The future of energy

CO_2 plays a critical role in maintaining the balance in the Earth's atmosphere and the air that we breathe. It is also a waste product of the fossil fuels that almost every person on the planet uses for transport and other energy requirements. Because we create CO_2 every time we drive a car, cook a meal or turn on a light, and because the gas lasts around a century in the atmosphere, the proportion of CO_2 in the atmosphere is rapidly increasing.

The best evidence indicates that we need to reduce carbon dioxide emissions by 70 per cent by 2050. If you own a four-wheel-drive car and replace it with a hybrid car – a car that is powered by a combination of electricity and petrol – or a smaller standard-fuel car, you can achieve a reduction of that magnitude in a day rather than half a century. Unfortunately, our past history of change is considerably slower than this. Samuel Bowser first invented the petrol pump in 1885 but it wasn't until 1988 that all new cars manufactured in the UK were required to use unleaded petrol only.

Not only do fossil fuels pose an environmental hazard but there is also a pressing need to find an alternative energy source that is renewable. Opinions as to how much oil remains vary considerably. Some say that the Earth has produced only 18 per cent of its potential yield of oil; others say supplies may run out as early as 2015. Many countries are exploring alternative energy sources such as solar energy or wind power, which uses large turbines to capture the energy of the wind.

1 How do you write CO_2 in full? ....

2 What do we call fuels such as coal and oil?
   ....

3 What are two names for the substance that comes out of the exhaust of a car? ....
   ....

4 What do we call fuels that can be produced at any time? ....

5 Name two types of alternative energy.
   ....

6 What is a turbine most similar to?
   A a large engine   B a windmill   C a car

Alternative fuels

2.2 Complete the text with words from the box.

alternative   converting   eco-friendly   emit   engine   fuel   fumes   greenhouse gases   plant   solar

Fueling our cars

Our love of the fuel-burning car with its poisonous exhaust (1)........................... has had a devastating effect both on our environment and on oil supplies. It is unlikely we will abandon our cars in large enough numbers to resolve this problem, so there is a pressing need to find an (2)........................... fuel. Many car companies are exploring (3)........................... energy sources. Hybrid cars were first developed in 1997 and these are likely to become more commonplace in the future. Hydrogen vehicles that use (4)........................... panels to extract hydrogen from water are also likely to be readily available in the near future. These vehicles (5)........................... only water vapour and so do not contribute to (6)........................... . However, critics say that building a network of fuelling stations and (7)........................... existing petrol stations to hydrogen will prove too costly and will limit this vehicle's potential. Nevertheless, countries such as the US, Germany, Japan and Iceland already have ambitious hydrogen plans.

Others believe that biofuels are the future. These fuels are based on (8)........................... oils and so can be grown. The concept of using vegetable oil as a (9)........................... dates back to 1895 when Dr Rudolf Diesel developed the first diesel (10)........................... to run on vegetable oil. He demonstrated his engine at the World Exhibition in Paris in 1900 and described an experiment using peanut oil as fuel in his engine. In 1912, Diesel said, 'The use of vegetable oils for engine fuels may seem insignificant today. But such oils may become in the course of time as important as petroleum and the coal tar products of the present time.'

> **Error warning!**
>
> *Gas* is the American word for *petrol*. *Smoke* is produced when
> something burns. *Fumes* are the gases produced by chemicals such as
> petrol: *Older cars generate a great deal of* **fumes**. NOT ~~*a great deal of*~~
> ~~*gas /a great deal of smoke*~~

2.3 **Decide whether these sentences are true or false. Underline the parts of the text that gave you your answer.**

1 Cars that run on electricity and petrol appeared in 1997. ....True...........

2 Water is produced from the exhausts of hydrogen cars. ....

3 It will be relatively inexpensive to change current petrol stations for hydrogen cars. ....

4 Biofuels are non-renewable. ....

5 In 1912 diesel was seen as an important fuel source. ....

2.4 **Which is the odd one out? Try to explain why.**

1 curb / limit / ~~promote~~ / restrict .The other words mean 'to reduce'............................

2 electricity / nuclear energy / solar energy / wind power ....

3 economical / effective / efficient / emission ....

4 carbon / fuel / gas / petrol ....

5 emit / discharge / release / retain ....

6 renewable / disposable / rechargeable ....

7 diminish / dwindle / deplete / drastic ....

8 consume / extend / exhaust / expend ....

9 conserve / preserve / reserve / save ....

2.5 **Answer these questions using as many new words and phrases from this unit as you can. If possible, record yourself and then listen to your answers.**

1 Do you think that you waste too much energy in the home?

2 What can the government do to encourage people to save energy?

3 Why do you think people prefer to drive a car instead of using public transport?

4 Do you feel optimistic about the future in terms of energy?

5 What changes do you think will happen in the next 20 years?

> **Test Tip**
>
> In the speaking test you will be assessed on your 'lexical resource'
> – in other words, whether you can use a wide range of vocabulary
> accurately. Think about your answers to these questions. Did you have
> to hesitate to search for words? Which words did you manage to use?
> Which words do you still need to practise?

Test practice

Academic Reading

America is abuzz with talk of replacing imported oil with 'biofuels' produced from homegrown materials. The US Environmental Protection Agency recently honoured famous country and western singer Willie Nelson for his efforts to promote the use of biodiesel through his own 'BioWillie' brand, a vegetable oil-based fuel which is now being distributed at filling stations nationally. Clearly, many hurdles stand in the way of making such biofuels commercially viable with traditional sources. Indeed, it remains very difficult to forecast whether powering our vehicles with crop derivatives will ever be a truly economic proposition. Nevertheless, it is not too early to ponder what impact the widespread adoption of biofuels would have on our environment.

Michael S. Briggs, a biodiesel advocate at the University of New Hampshire, has estimated that the United States would need about 140 billion gallons of biodiesel each year to replace all the petroleum-based transportation fuels currently being used. This calculation is premised on the idea that Americans could, over time, switch to using diesel vehicles, as European drivers are clearly doing – half of the new cars sold there now run on standard diesel. Although one could make a similar appraisal for the amount of sugar-derived ethanol needed to meet our needs, it is unlikely that drivers would ever want to fill up their tanks entirely with ethanol, which contains only two-thirds of the energy of gasoline, whereas biodiesel is only 2 per cent less fuel-efficient than petroleum-based diesel. Hence a switch to biofuels would demand no new technology and would not significantly reduce the driving range of a car or truck.

The main source of biodiesel is plant oil derived from crops such as rapeseed. An acre of rapeseed could provide about 100 gallons of biodiesel per year. To fuel America in this way would thus require 1.4 billion acres of rapeseed fields. This number is a sizeable fraction of the total US land area (2.4 billion acres) and considerably more than the 400 million acres currently under cultivation. Consequently, the burden on freshwater supplies and the general disruption that would accompany such a switch in fuel sources would be immense.

Such calculations are sobering. They suggest that weaning ourselves off petroleum fuels and growing rapeseed instead would be an environmental catastrophe. Are more productive oil crops the answer? Oil palms currently top the list because they can provide enough oil to produce about 500 gallons of biodiesel per acre per year, which reduces the land requirement fivefold. Yet its cultivation demands a tropical climate, and its large-scale production, which currently comes from such countries as Malaysia and Indonesia, is a significant factor in the ongoing destruction of what rainforest remains there. Conservationists have been warning that palm oil production poses a dire threat to the dwindling population of orang-utans, for example, which exist only in the wild in Borneo and Sumatra. So here again, the prospect of dedicating sufficient land to growing feedstock for the world's transportation needs promises to be an environmental nightmare.

There is, however, a 'crop' that is widely recognised as having the potential to meet the demands of a biodiesel-based transportation fleet without devastating the natural landscape: algae. Algae is a single-celled plant, some varieties of which can contain 50 per cent or more oil. They also grow much more rapidly than ordinary plants and can double in quantity within several hours.

The US Department of Energy funded considerable research on biofuel production using algae after the oil problems of the 1970s, an effort known as the Aquatic Species Program. Although this programme was terminated in the 1990s, a lot of experience was gained through research and various demonstration projects. The results suggested that algae can be grown in sufficient density to produce several thousand gallons of biodiesel per acre per year – a full order of magnitude better than can be expected using palm oil and two orders of magnitude better than soybeans.

It is not surprising then that many scientists and entrepreneurs are once again looking hard at the prospects for using algae to produce transportation fuels and sizeable amounts of money are being invested in various schemes for doing so. David Bayless, a professor of mechanical engineering at Ohio University, has been working with scientists to engineer a device that can grow cyanobacteria (blue-green algae). It uses carbon dioxide from the gases emitted from power-plant chimneys and sunlight that is distributed to the growing surfaces through optical fibres. Bayless uses an enclosed bioreactor and claims to be able to produce as much as 60 grams of biomass per square metre of growing surface per day.

Another recent effort is being carried out in San Diego by KentSeaTech Corporation. This company gained experience growing algae as a part of its aquaculture operations so was quick to respond when the California state government started looking for ways to treat the huge quantities of nutrient-laden water which runs off from adjacent farm lands. 'It's no real difficult feat to turn nutrients into algae,' says director of research Jon Van Olst, 'but how do you get it out of the water?' This is what Van Olst and his co-workers have been trying to achieve.

The people working on these ventures are clearly eager to make growing algae a commercial success. Yet it is not hard to find experts who view such prospects as dim indeed. John Benemann, a private consultant in California, has decades of experience in this area. He is particularly sceptical about attempts to make algae production more economical by using enclosed bioreactors rather than open ponds. He points out that Japan spent hundreds of millions of dollars on such research, which never went anywhere. Even Van Olst has serious reservations. 'It may work,' he says, 'but it is going to take a while and a lot of research before we get anywhere.'

Questions 1–5

Classify the following characteristics as belonging to
   A   biodiesel
   B   ethanol
   C   ordinary diesel

Write the correct answers A–C next to questions 1–5.

1   Produced by a popular American entertainer. ....

2   50% of new cars in Europe use this fuel. ....

3   Provides two thirds of the power of standard petrol. ....

4   Your car's performance will be almost unchanged if you change to this fuel. ....

5   Production can have a negative impact on water resources. ....

Questions 6–12

Do the following statements agree with the claims of the writer in the reading passage?

Next to questions 6–12 write
    Yes   if the statement agrees with the claims of the writer
    No   if the statement contradicts the claims of the writer
    Not given   if it is impossible to say what the writer thinks about this

6   2% of Americans already use biodiesel. ....

7   At present in America, 400 million acres of land are used for agriculture. ....

8   The use of palm oil as a fuel source will require more land than using rapeseed oil. ....

9   Growing biodiesel crops has had a positive effect on local wildlife in some areas. ....

10 One advantage of algae is the speed with which it grows. ....

11 David Bayless believes that algae can produce more energy than solar power. ....

12 It is easy to grow algae using agricultural waste water. ....

Question 13

Choose the correct answer **A**, **B**, **C** or **D**.

13 What is the main purpose of this article?
    A   To prove that biofuels could totally replace petrol in America.
    B   To examine the environmental impact of standard fuel sources.
    C   To assess the advantages and disadvantages of different types of fuel.
    D   To show that an international effort is required to solve the fuel crisis.

17 Talking business

Employment, management and marketing

Employment

1.1 Answer these questions.

Have you ever worked in any of these places? If not, would you like to?

A a shop   B a restaurant   C a hotel   D an office

1.2 🎧 17a Listen and match the speakers to the correct industry. Write your answers in the second column. In the third column, write the adjectives the speakers use to describe their job.

advertising
building
hospitality
retail

Speaker	Type of industry	Adjectives used to describe work
1		
2		
3		
4		

1.3 🎧 17a Complete the sentences with words from the recording. If necessary, listen to the speakers again.

1 I'm employed on a casual basis, so my .... are paid at the end of each week.

2 Over 100 members of staff were made .... when the new machines were installed in the factory.

3 It is important to have experience in the .... as well as academic qualifications.

4 I do .... so I often have to sleep during the day.

5 The owners had a meeting with all of the .... to discuss the takeover.

6 The government may decide to raise the age at which people .... from work from 65 to 70.

7 My boss has asked me to work .... tomorrow, so I won't be home until late.

8 Our junior staff .... $12 per hour.

9 If they don't increase my .... this year then I'm going to look for another job.

10 Many young people today value .... over a big salary.

1.4 Complete the sentences using the correct form of the word *employ*.

1 The .... find it difficult to get an interview if they have not had a job for a long time.

2 All .... must apply in writing if they wish to request a holiday.

3 .... rose by 5 per cent due to the closure of two large factories in the area.

4 I was only............................... as a cleaner, but the family expected me to look after their children as well.

5 I couldn't work when my daughter was sick. Fortunately, my .... is very understanding.

Vocabulary note

A *job* = the particular thing you do to earn money: *I'm hoping to get **a job** during the holidays.*
Occupation = a formal word for *job*.
Profession = a type of job that requires specialist knowledge: *He works in the medical **profession**.*
Work = something you do to earn money. It is a verb as well as an uncountable noun: *I'm hoping to find **work** during the holidays.* NOT ~~find a work.~~
Workforce = all the people working in a company/industry/country: *A company is only as good as its **workforce**.*
Workplace = the building or room where people work: *You really need experience in the **workplace** to get a good job.*

Management and marketing

2.1 Think of a word or phrase that matches the definitions below.

1   The business or trade in a particular product. m...............................
2   People who buy goods. c...............................
3   The materials in which objects are wrapped before being sold. p...............................
4   A new fashion or pattern of behaviour. t...............................
5   When someone can be believed or trusted. c...............................
6   Make someone do something by giving them a good reason to do it. p...............................
7   A means of identifying a particular company. b...............................
8   The things a company makes to sell. p...............................

2.2 Now read the following text and check your answers to 2.1.

Luxury brands dominate both the cosmetic and skincare market. But consumers are looking for more than just beauty in sophisticated packaging. Companies offering products with healthy ingredients have set the trend in recent years. When consumers go shopping for cosmetics, they want to know the products they are buying won't harm their skin. To gain credibility, many cosmetic companies have persuaded dermatologists and pharmacists to endorse their brands. The target customers of most skincare and cosmetic brands are women between the ages of 20 and 50, a segment that is only expected to grow in the coming years. Nevertheless, men are also looking for products to give their skin a healthy look. It is estimated that men account for 1 per cent of the luxury cosmetics market, a niche which saw a 50 per cent increase in sales in 2003–04. Besides men, teenagers are also trying to enhance the health and beauty of their appearance. With such a broad client base, it is not surprising that the industry shows no sign of slowing down.

Error warning!

Products is used to refer to things that are produced to be sold – the focus is on the company producing them. *Goods* is used to refer to things that are sold – the focus is on the buying or selling of these. *Goods* cannot be used in the singular. *We have tested each **product**.* NOT ~~We have tested each goods/good.~~

3.1 **Use a dictionary to check the meaning of the words in the box. Then choose the correct words in the sentences.**

income   salary   wages   earnings

1   Buying larger containers of food is a more *economic / economical* way of shopping.

2   I would like to increase my *income / money* so I'm going to invest in some shares.

3   I need to earn more *money / income* so that I can buy that new computer.

4   Nowadays people worry a great deal about *earnings / money*.

5   My *earnings / money* increased by 10 per cent last year.

> **Error warning!**
>
> *Economical* = something that does not use a lot of fuel or money: *My new car is really economical to use. Economic* = the money of a country: *A strong government needs good **economic** policies.* NOT *economical policies*

> **Vocabulary note**
>
> *Advertisement* or *advert* = a picture or short film used to persuade people to buy a product or apply for a job: *Did you see the **advertisement** in the paper? Advertising* = the business of trying to persuade people to buy things.

3.2 **Correct the mistakes in the text.**

There is little that parents and teachers can do to help young adults to prepare themselves for the workforce. Do you agree?

The number of [1]*unemployment* seems to increase each year and the competition for each [2]*work* is also increasing. Consequently, young adults need to do as much as they can to prepare to enter the [3]*working place*. There are several things that children can do at school and at home to help them.

Firstly, once they reach 15 or 16 years of age, children should be encouraged to plan their [4]*profession*. No matter what [5]*work* they choose, choosing early will help them to make sure they learn the appropriate [6]*knowledge* during their studies. For example, if they choose a [7]*work* in the [8]*advertisement* industry, it can help if they study the arts. Teachers can also help by showing children the best way to respond to an [9]*advertising* for a job.

At home, parents can teach children how to stick to a budget. If a country experiences an [10]*economical crisis*, these skills are invaluable. They can begin by making children [11]*gain* their pocket money by doing [12]*job* in the home. They could even be paid more or less [13]*earnings* based on the quality of their [14]*job*. If children develop a strong work ethic from an early age then this should ensure that they have enough money when they reach [15]*retire* age.

1   *unemployed*   6   11   ....
2   7   12   ....
3   8   13   ....
4   9   14   ....
5   10   15   ....

4.1 **PRONUNCIATION** 🔊 17b **Which words are pronounced in a similar way? Put the words in the box into the correct column according to their sound. Then listen and check. Practise saying the words.**

clerk   earn   first   floor   force   law
market   nurse   perk   poor   purse
target   walk   work

ɜː	ɑː	ɔː
bird	park	ball

Test practice

General Training Writing Task 1

You should spend about 20 minutes on this task.

You work in a busy but poorly organised office and you are keep to be promoted. Your employer needs to find a new supervisor for your department.

Write a letter to your employer. In the letter
- **ask to be considered for this job**
- **explain why you would be a suitable candidate**
- **outline the current problems and the changes you would like to make.**

You should write at least 150 words.
You do **NOT** need to write any addresses.
Begin your letter as follows:

Dear Mr Smith

> **Test Tip**
>
> Make sure that you address each of the bullet points. Use your own words instead of copying from the question paper. When you have finished, check your spelling and make sure you have written at least 150 words. Study the information in unit 25 before you begin.

Academic Writing Task 2

You should spend about 40 minutes on this task.

Present a written argument or case to an educated reader with no specialist knowledge of the following topic.

In today's job market it is far more important to have practical skills than theoretical knowledge. In the future, job applicants may not need any formal qualifications.

To what extent do you agree or disagree?

You should use your own ideas, knowledge and experience and support your arguments with examples and relevant evidence.

Write at least 250 words.

> **Test Tip**
>
> Make sure that you address each of the points in the question. Use your own words instead of copying words from the question paper. When you have finished, check your spelling and make sure you have written at least 250 words. Study the information in unit 24 before you begin.

18 The law
Crime, punishment

Crime

1.1 Put the following into order from least to most serious. Which do you think are considered to be crimes?

arson   burglary   fraud   vandalism
kidnapping   murder   pickpocketing
smuggling   swearing   dumping toxic waste

1.2 Now read the text and decide whether statements 1–7 are true or false. Write the words from the text which mean the same as or the opposite of the words in *italics*.

Crime

Crime is defined by society and relative to the society defining it. Traditionally, crime is considered an offence, a violation of public rules or laws. Crime is defined within each society by specific criminal laws on a national, state and local level. Actions that are offensive to an individual or group of people, but do not violate laws are not crimes. Punishment or other sanctions result from the violation of these laws, and the social system for monitoring and enforcing public rules or laws is put into action. The social system generally consists of an administrative authority that formally deals with crime and a force of representative officers to enforce the laws and act on behalf of society. Being guilty of a criminal act usually involves some form of conscious evil intent or recklessness. In unintentional cases, such as crimes committed by children or the insane, the criminal is not usually punished in the same manner as is intentional crime.

Theories of crime and criminal activity are numerous and varied, but the reasons behind crime remain elusive. Theories suggest many possible causes. One theory suggests that property crime depends on criminal motive and opportunities to perpetrate crime. It also contends that crime is influenced by the degree to which others guard over neighbourhoods and other people. This particular theory relates an increase in crime rate to an increase in crime opportunity and a decrease in protection. Research also shows that income inequality correlates to property crime.

1   Offence is another word for crime. ....*True – crime is considered an offence*....

2   The word offensive is related to crime. ....

3   It is the duty of the police to *violate* the law. ....

4   Generally, people who are guilty of a crime are *aware* of what they are doing. ....

5   The explanations for crime are *difficult to find*. ....

6   Crime can increase if people *protect* their property less. ....

7   Crime on property *is linked* to the different amounts of money people earn. ....

1.3 WORD BUILDING Complete the table.

Noun	Verb	Adjective
crime	c........................ a crime	
	deter	
	enforce	
	offend	
prevention		
prison		
punishment		

> **Error warning!**
>
> A _convict_ is a person who is in prison. To _convict_ someone is to find them guilty in a court of law. You _commit a crime_ or _convict a criminal_, not ~~convict a crime~~. We talk about _criminal acts_, NOT ~~criminal actions~~

1.4 Complete the sentences with a suitable word from the table in **1.3**.

1 All .... acts should be punished.

2 Every society needs a strong system of law ....

3 People who .... crimes are often victims themselves.

4 I think dumping toxic waste should be made a .... offence. There is little to .... people from doing this at the moment.

5 I think we could have .... this crime by fitting an extra lock on the door.

Punishment

2.1 Match the verbs in column A with the nouns in column B.

A	B
accept	a crime
commit	a law
convict	a fine
impose	the consequences
pass	a criminal

2.2 Match the people with the things they do.

List of people

1 The accused = ..C..

2 The judge ....

3 The jury ....

4 The prosecutor ....

5 The lawyer ....

6 The victim ....

List of things they do

A ... tries to prove the accused is guilty.

B ... gives evidence against the accused.

C ... the person who is on trial.

D ... decides whether the accused is innocent or guilty.

E ... tries to prove the accused is innocent.

F ... decides how a criminal should be punished.

2.3 COLLOCATION **What words can you use with** *crime* **and** *law*? **Write in the boxes below.**

	Crime	Law
Adjectives	serious	
Verbs		

2.4 🔊 18 **Now listen and fill in any blanks you have in the table.**

2.5 🔊 18 **Complete the sentences with suitable words from the recording. You may need to change the grammatical form of the word. Listen and check your answers.**

1 I consider myself to be a law-a......................... citizen. I've never broken the law in my life.

2 The laws in this country are rather s......................... – even chewing gum is banned.

3 Arson is a crime a......................... property, but sometimes people can get hurt as well.

4 I was given a parking f......................... again yesterday. It's costing me a fortune.

5 It is the responsibility of the police and the government to c......................... crime.

6 More money should be spent on crime p......................... than on building prisons.

7 Sometimes the police feel that they are a......................... the law and should not be punished for traffic offences.

8 It used to be against the law to go fishing on Sundays, but thankfully that law was a......................... years ago.

> **Ⓥ** *Vocabulary note*
>
> *Prevent* = to stop something from happening or someone from doing something: *I stayed away from the bully to **prevent** any trouble. This will **prevent** crimes from happening.* NOT ~~*This will avoid crimes*~~
> *Avoid* = to stay away from someone or something: *You should try to **avoid** dangerous situations.*

3.1 **Correct the mistakes in the text.**

'Our prison system is clearly not working. We need to find another form of punishment.'

If people ¹*convict* a crime then they should be punished and made to accept the consequences of their ²*acts*. At the moment the only form of ³*punish* we have is to either ⁴*find* people for ⁵*small* crimes or ⁶*emprison* them for more serious criminal ⁷*offend*.

Some people feel that this system is not working. Perhaps this is because ⁸*the bad people* mix with other ⁹*crimes* when they are in jail. As a result, prisons may provide a way for young people who have been involved ¹⁰*for* minor offences to graduate to ¹¹*bigger* ones.

Rather than trying to ¹²*prevent* this problem by building even more prisons, I believe the best approach is to try to ¹³*avoid* crime from happening in the first place. We can do this by making sure that our property is ¹⁴*protection* and also by improving the conditions for the poorer people in our society. We can also achieve this by ¹⁵*making* new laws that will act as a ¹⁶*deter*.

1	Commit	5	....	9	....	13	....
2	....	6	....	10	....	14	....
3	....	7	....	11	....	15	....
4	....	8	....	12	....	16	....

Test practice

General Training Writing Task 2

You should spend about 40 minutes on this task.

Write about the following topic.

In many countries the level of crime is increasing and crimes are becoming more violent.

Why do you think this is and what can be done about it?

Give reasons for your answer and include any relevant examples from your experience.

You should write at least 250 words.

Test Tip

Use the space below to make a plan before you begin to write so that you can organise your ideas logically. Do not try to learn any essays by heart. When you have finished, check your spelling and make sure you have written at least 250 words. Study the information in unit 25 before you begin.

Test Tip

This essay question is also good practice for Academic Writing Task 2.

....
....
....
....
....
....
....
....
....
....
....
....
....
....
....
....
....
....
....
....
....

19 The media

The news, fame

The news

1.1 **Answer these questions.**

1 Are you
   A well-informed about current affairs?
   B not interested in current affairs?

2 Do you consider newspapers to be
   A biased   B entertaining   C informative?

3 Do you prefer to get the news from
   A newspapers   B the Internet   C the radio   D the television?

1.2 🔊 **19a** **Listen and say whether the following statements are true or false according to the speaker. Correct the statements that are false.**

1 The speaker believes the general public is well-informed. .... *False, they are ill-informed.*

2 The Manly University project focused on stories about famous people.

   ....

3 Dan Taylor believes that the main aim of today's mass media is to inform people.

   ....

4 The study revealed that newspapers avoid reporting on the gap between the rich and the poor.

   ....

5 Important news stories appear in the back pages because this highlights their importance.

   ....

1.3 🔊 **19a** **Listen again and find words or phrases that match these definitions.**

1 a situation in which newspapers, radio and television are allowed to express opinions openly

2 to send out a programme on television or radio

3 written about or spoken of in the news

4 large systems consisting of many similar parts all of which are centrally controlled

5 newspapers, radio and television when seen as a group

6 the deliberate removal of sections of a text or film considered to be unsuitable

7 a popular newspaper with lots of pictures and short articles

8 words in large print at the start of a news story or the main stories in the news

1.4 Read the following information about the same story and complete the text with words from the box.

biased   controversial   exposés   front page   publications   press   safeguards   sources

In response to the study, Martin Dexter from the Associated Press said: "This study seems to be rather a harsh attack on the [1]............................ and I can't agree with its conclusions. You need to remember that we have a broad range of media sources available to us nowadays. There is an enormous amount of alternative media that provide a healthy balance to the mainstream. If people want to be informed, they are unlikely to turn to tabloid newspapers to do so. Instead, they can access a wide range of journals, magazines and smaller [2]............................ . They can also search the Web for the most up-to-date information from any part of the world. On the negative side, there is a problem with editor verification with some stories reported on the internet because [3]............................ can be unreliable. The [4]............................ in place for traditional media just don't exist there at the moment."

"I'll admit that stories about [5]............................ issues are less likely to be seen by the tabloids as [6].................. .... news. But I would be more concerned about content which is politically [7]............................ or motivated. I believe there are many publishers and broadcasters that do still have a strong tradition of [8]............................ and investigative journalism. If there is an emphasis on entertainment rather than more serious issues, then this is being driven by consumer demand. Perhaps ultimately we only get the media we deserve."

1.5 Now answer these questions.

1   What do we call newspapers when seen as a group?

2   What is the opposite of mainstream media?

3   What is another word for the Internet?

4   What does Martin Dexter believe is the problem with new media?

5   What do we call the type of journalism that tries to discover the truth behind issues that are of public interest?

Fame

2.1 Use a dictionary to check the meaning of these verbs. Find out the noun and adjective forms and write them in your notebook.

bias   exploit   expose   inform   intrude   invade   investigate
publish   publicise   sensationalise   verify

2.2 Use a suitable form of the words in **2.1** to replace the words in bold.

1   There has been a lot of **gossip** .... *speculation* .... in the media about the identity of the victim.

2   Not surprisingly, the reporter was unable to **prove the truth behind** .... the claims.

3   The government has agreed to launch an official **inquiry** .... into the matter.

4   There has been a great deal of **media hype** .... about the new James Bond movie.

5   I'm not sure celebrities are being **used** ...., they often seem to court fame.

6   Most people believe that this newspaper favours the government too much to provide an **impartial** .... coverage of the election.

> ### Ⓥ Vocabulary note
>
> We say something/someone **has a / is a** *good/bad/positive* or *negative*
> **influence on** someone/something: *John's new friends* **are a** *really bad*
> **influence on** *him. Influence can be a verb or a noun: The media* **influences**
> *the way many people think. The media* **has a** *major* **influence on** *the way
> many people think.*
> Remember that *effect* is a noun and *affect* is a verb. These can be used in
> a similar way to *influence: The media* **affects** *the way many people think.
> The media* **has a** *major* **effect on** *the way many people think.*

> ### Error warning!
>
> We say **on** *the radio,* **on** *television,*
> **on** *screen,* **on** *the computer,* **on** *the
> Internet. We use* **in** *with printed
> media: We learn all about celebrities*
> **in** *magazines or* **on** *television.* NOT
> *~~in magazines or television~~. These
> materials are freely available* **on** *the
> Internet.* NOT *~~in the Internet~~.*

3.1 These adjectives can be used to talk about the media or people in the media. Decide whether they are used
in a negative or a positive way and put them in the correct box.

artificial   biased   distorted   factual
informative   invasive   intrusive
pervasive   realistic   sensationalist
superficial   unbiased   attention-grabbing

Positive	*Negative*

3.2 Think about your answers to these questions. Try to use as many of the adjectives from **3.1** as you can.

1   Would you like to be famous? (Why? / Why not?)

2   Do you think famous people have a positive or a negative influence on young people?

3   Nowadays we have access to the news 24 hours a day. What effect does this have?

3.3 🎧 19b Complete these answers to the questions in **3.2** with a suitable word or phrase. Then listen and check
your answers.

1   I think a lot of people want to be famous nowadays and that's why reality TV is so popular. But I wouldn't like
to be famous at all. Being famous nowadays simply means that you're in the ¹t.............................. a lot and you're
followed by the ²p............................. everywhere you go. I'd find that very ³i............................. . Famous people
have no ⁴p............................. at all in any part of their life. Their life also seems to be very ⁵s.............................
because they spend all of their time going to parties and trying to look glamorous. It all seems very
⁶a............................. to me – they just don't seem to be part of the real world at all.

2   I think they should have a positive ⁷i............................. on young people, but many of them don't. Some
personalities are good role models and use their ⁸c............................. status to encourage people to think about
important issues, but we often see photos of famous people behaving badly.

3   I think it can ⁹a............................. us in both positive and negative ways. On the one hand, it's very convenient to
be able to catch up with what's happening in the world at any time of the day or night, no matter where you are.
But on the other hand, this kind of news can give you a ¹⁰d............................. view of what's happening, because
even minor news ¹¹s............................. are given more importance than they perhaps should have.

4.1 PRONUNCIATION Which of the following sounds do these words have: s (<u>s</u>top), z (<u>z</u>oo), ʒ (A<u>s</u>ia) or ʃ (<u>sh</u>op)?

artif<u>ici</u>al ..ʃ...   cen<u>s</u>or ....   intru<u>s</u>ive ....   inva<u>s</u>ive ....
atten<u>ti</u>on ....   expo<u>s</u>ed ....   intru<u>s</u>ion ....   publica<u>ti</u>on ....
bia<u>s</u>ed ....   expo<u>s</u>ure ....   inva<u>s</u>ion ....   superfi<u>ci</u>al ....

4.2 🎧 19c Now listen and practise saying the words.

Test practice

Academic Writing Task 2

You should spend about 40 minutes on this task.

Present a written argument or case to an educated reader with no specialist knowledge of the following topic.

Whoever controls the media also controls opinions and attitudes of the people and there is little that can be done to rectify this.

To what extent do you agree or disagree?

You should use your own ideas, knowledge and experience and support your arguments with examples and relevant evidence.

Write at least 250 words.

Test Tip

Use the space below to make a plan before you begin to write so that you can organise your ideas logically. Do not try to learn any essays by heart. When you have finished, check your spelling and make sure you have written at least 250 words. Study the information in unit 24 before you begin.

....
....
....
....
....
....
....
....
....
....
....
....
....
....
....
....
....
....
....
....

20 The arts
Art appreciation, the performing arts

Art appreciation

1.1 Which art forms are shown in these pictures?
What do we call the people who do these things?

1.2 Which of these art forms do you find the most and least appealing?

1.3 Read the text making sure you understand the meaning of the words in bold. Use a dictionary if necessary.

The brain of the beholder

The cave figures of Lascaux, Leonardo da Vinci's *Mona Lisa*, a Cubist painting by Pablo Picasso and the African **artefact** that **inspired** Picasso's work. These works of art are separated by great gulfs in time, different social and political systems, and language divides. Yet despite these variations, there is art in each place and era. That there is a seemingly **universal impulse** to express oneself this way suggests that human beings are neurologically hardwired for art.

Imagine yourself in the Louvre in Paris, pushing through the throngs to behold the Mona Lisa's enigmatic smile. Or recall the first time you ever saw the Sydney Opera House. Most likely your skin tingled, you felt a thrill and you paused for a moment of **reflection**. Even glimpses of **mundane** objects such as the latest curvaceous kettle, can inspire something similar. Art and design critics will describe how formal qualities like proportion are **choreographed** to produce the viewer's **rush**. But the fact that **aesthetic** experience can inspire such a biological response suggests that it's a stimulus neuroscientists could analyse just as **deftly**.

And that's exactly what they are doing. In laboratories and galleries around the world, researchers are showing how the organisation of the brain relates to the **conception** and experience of art. This is the **burgeoning** field of neuroaesthetics, in which scientists are discovering that – rather than **transcending** the ordinary – art and aesthetics are part of everyday experience. They're also finding that, in some **fundamental** ways, art really is an expression of human nature.

1.4 Write *Yes* if these statements agree with the information in the text or *No* if the statements contradict the information. Write the words in bold that helped you with your answer.

1 Pablo Picasso got the idea for one of his paintings from an ancient work of art from Africa.
   Yes – artefact, inspired

2 The desire to create art is limited to certain parts of the world. ....

3 When people look at works of art it provokes serious and careful thought. ....

4 Ordinary objects can be aesthetically pleasing. ....

5 Art critics believe that artistic elements are arranged and combined together in order to create a feeling of excitement. ....

6 Researchers are analysing how the brain creates the idea of art. ....

7 Neuroaesthetics is failing to catch on in the world of science. ....

8 Scientists have discovered that art is a way of rising above everyday life. ....

The performing arts

2.1 [🎧 20a] You will hear a radio broadcast about three different arts festivals on Bethania island. Listen and complete column A below. Write **NO MORE THAN ONE WORD** for each answer.

A	B
Living (1) ....**– Week**	1 *the study of art in relation to its beauty =* ....
• Talks	
• (2) .... lunches	2 *organised sets of special events =* ....
• Book (3)	
• (4) .... for children	
• This year's (5) .... is Island Life	
The (6) .... **Arts**	3 *skilled =* ....
• A painting (7)	4 *creations =* ....
• Discussion of the (8) .... process	5 *represent or show something in a picture or story =* ....
• Workshops at local (9)	6 *make shapes in wood or stone with a knife =* ....
• Display of local (10)	
• (11) .... **of Voices**	7 *describes a show that involves the audience =* ....
• Several performances will be (12)	8 *the people gathered to listen to a performance =* ....
• (13) .... theatre	9 *take part in =* ....
• Free (14)	10 *musical performances =* ....

2.2 [🎧 20a] Now listen again and find words or phrases to match the definitions in column B.

2.3 WORD BUILDING Complete the table.

Noun	Verb	Adjective
		creative
culture		
	influence	
	inspire	
imagination		
	participate	
		rich

3.1 Try to talk for two minutes about the following topic. Use words from the table in **2.3** if you can.

> Describe the type of music that you like. You should say
> - why you enjoy listening to this type of music
> - the times or places when you listen to this music
> - your feelings about music in general and say whether you prefer live or recorded music.

3.2 (🎧 20b) You will hear somebody answering the question in **3.1**. Listen and complete the text with no more than two words from the text. You may need to listen twice.

My taste in music is quite [1] .... and there isn't really one [2] .... of music that I like. I listen to everything from [3] .... music to [4] .... Music [5] .... a very important [6] .... in my life, and I listen to it almost constantly. I find that it helps to [7] .... or to change a [8] .... So I tend to choose my music according to who I'm with or what I'm doing. For example, if I'm driving long distances in my car I prefer to play something [9] .... to help keep me awake, but if I'm having a dinner party with friends then I play something more [10] .... I think that music helps to [11] .... me when I'm working, although my colleagues find it [12] .... so I tend to listen with [13] .... on. In that way I can [14] .... into my own little world. When I was younger I would definitely have said that I preferred live music. The [15] .... in a live [16] .... can be [17] .... Nowadays, though, a lot of popular groups only perform at very large [18] .... in front of [19] .... of 20,000 or more and I don't really like that. I prefer the [20] .... of listening to recorded music, and the sound quality is better as well. Music really [21] .... our lives – it can turn a boring, monotonous period of time into a [22] .... So I think it's essential to have music and, in fact, all of [23] .... in your life.

4 PRONUNCIATION (🎧 20c) Each of the following words has a weak sound or *schwa* (ə), e.g. *about*. <u>Underline</u> the weak sounds in each word then listen and check your answers. Practise saying the words. There may be more than one schwa in each word.

atmosphere	classical	edition	festival	fundamental	imagination
literary	monotonous	musical	performance	popular	visual

Test practice

Academic Reading

You should spend about 20 minutes on questions 1–12, which are based on the reading passage.

Storytelling

Dr Tom Sjöblom, University of Helsinki, explores the link between narratives and memories.

Storytelling seems to be a fundamental feature of human existence. In a recent article, Paul Hernadi points out that storytelling and narratives are such widespread phenomena that they could justifiably be included in the list of human universals (Hernadi, 2001). But, our craving for narratives, or stories, goes deeper than this. It is embedded in our mental images of whatever happens around us (Boyer, 2001). In other words, creating narratives is our way of connecting and interacting with our environment (Mink, 1978).

As a species, we humans appear to have a much more active attitude towards our environment than any other species. Our bodies and minds not only adapt to the surrounding world, but we actively shape and construct our environment to better suit our needs (Plotkin, 1993). From this perspective, culture is nothing more than an environment that we create ourselves. Culture is not something in opposition to nature. Instead it is a part of it, it is – in a way – nature modified to better suit the requirements of the human life form. Thus, culture and all aspects of it are basically products of natural selection and, more specifically, the evolution of the human mind (Boyer, 2001).

Between 60,000 and 20,000 years ago the first signs of art and religion appeared and humans started to build houses and invent more sophisticated tools and weapons, such as bows and arrows. This period has been called the 'big bang' of human culture. There is still much controversy over how to explain this period of innovation, but a growing consensus connects the greater cultural energy and innovation of the period to the emergence of individuals as creative beings (Mellars, 1994).

The archaeologist Steven Mithen has suggested that this creativity can be explained by the emergence of a 'cognitively fluid' mentality, in other words, an ability to link together information from different areas of our life. Cognitive fluidity makes it possible for human beings to emerge from the concrete situational present and to adopt a more general and abstract approach (Mithen, 1996). As Gerald Edelman puts it: 'With that ability come the abilities to model the world, to make explicit comparisons and to weigh outcomes; through such comparisons comes the possibility of reorganizing plans.' (Edelman, 1992)

Edelman goes further than this and argues that it is the flexibility of our memory system which is the key for understanding how cognitive fluidity affects our ability to learn new things in general (Edelman, 1992). The basic idea here is that our memory does not really represent the past as it happened. In most of the cases it does not even represent it as it is stored and coded into our brains. Instead, our memory prefers creating the past from the perspective of how relevant it is to our present situation. Striving for this kind of coherence, our mind combines stored representations and blends information stored in them (Holyoak & Thagard, 1995). Thus, all things being equal, we do not remember the past, we create it.

The medieval art of memory, known as *memoria*, has interested historians for a long time, but seldom from a psychological or cognitive perspective. Recently, this has been changed through the work of Mary Carruthers. According to Carruthers, *memoria* was the reason why literature, in a fundamental sense, existed in medieval Europe. It was the process by which a work of literature became both institutionalised by the group and learned by its individual members (Carruthers, 1990).

For those medieval experts who were educated in the art of memory there were two principal strategies for achieving their goal. The first and older of these strategies, attributed to Aristotle, relied on the concept of 'mental images'. Supporters of this strategy argued that remembering was to see mental pictures, which are firmly imprinted upon the memory. Thus, the best way to memorise narratives is to stimulate the act of memorising by using visual aids such as emotion-provoking representations, or so-called 'word pictures'. Descriptive language can also be used to create a kind of mental painting, although no actual pictures are present (Carruthers, 1990). As Albertus Magnus (1193–1280) puts it: 'something is not secure enough by hearing, but it is made firm by seeing' (Albertus I.1. ll. 6–7).

The second, and more popular, strategy for memorising narratives was by rote learning. This was achieved by the frequent repetition of a text until it was accurately memorised. In this case, the process of memorising was aided by the use of rhythmic and/or formulaic expressions, and by breaking longer texts into numbered segments and then memorising them one by one (Carruthers, 1990).

The followers of this strategy criticised the use of visual imagery because of its inaccuracy. It was argued that the use of visual aids was marginally helpful at best, providing cues for recollection, but could not in itself guarantee the accuracy of the memorising process (Carruthers, 1990). The latter countered the criticism by arguing that, while in ordinary circumstances the accuracy of visual imagery could not be trusted, this problem would disappear if the visual imagery was strong enough to make a person emotionally engaged with the text. Indeed, they argued, it is the creation of strong emotional responses that makes the use of visual images such a powerful tool for memory creation (Carruthers, 1990).

Questions 1–8

Look at the following theories (questions 1–8) and the list of people below.
Match each person with the correct theory.
Write the correct letter (A–H) next to questions 1–8.

1 Early European storytelling came about because of a traditional form of memorising. ....

2 Cognitive fluidity allowed early humans to make and change arrangements. ....

3 Telling stories allows us to relate to our surroundings. ....

4 The brain changes our recollection of past events to match our current circumstances. ....

5 Telling stories is a trait which is common to all nations. ....

6 Early humans became more inventive when they were able to make a connection between different ideas. ....

7 Your memory of something will be improved if you visualise it rather than just listen to it. ....

8   Humans adjust to their surroundings as well as changing them. ....

```
              List of people
 A  Hernadi         E  Edelman
 B  Mink            F  Holyoak & Thagard
 C  Plotkin         G  Carruthers
 D  Mithen          H  Albertus
```

Questions 9–12

Complete each sentence with the correct ending **A–F** from the box.
Write the correct letter **(A–F)** next to questions 9–12.

 9 Those who memorised using Aristotle's theory were helped by ....

10 The experts who used rote learning were helped by ....

11 Those who supported rote learning believed that ....

12 Supporters of Aristotle's method of memorising believed that ....

```
 A  ...writing down their stories.
 B  ...using paintings aided the memory.
 C  ...visual aids were of limited help when memorising text.
 D  ...if images evoked a passionate response then the memory would be more accurate.
 E  ...creating a vivid image in their mind.
 F  ...turning a long text into a series of short parts.
```

Test Four (Units 16–20)

Choose the correct letter A, B, C or D.

1   People would use a lot less power if they bought household goods that were energy..................... .
    A effective   **B** efficient   **C** economical   **D** ecological

2   The .... from car exhausts have a significant effect on global warming.
    A emissions   **B** smoke   **C** gases   **D** acid

3   Our greatest problem is that we are .... more and more fossil fuels each year and supplies are dwindling.
    A conserving   **B** consuming   **C** producing   **D** preserving

4   We need to persuade people to change their habits so that they .... more energy.
    A consume   **B** conserve   **C** produce   **D** use

5   In the future we will need to use .... energy sources such solar power.
    A recycled   **B** reinvented   **C** renewable   **D** reusable

6   If oil supplies run out in 2015 then we need to find .... energy sources soon.
    A alternate   **B** alternating   **C** alternative   **D** altering

7   I need to earn a lot more .... before I can afford to buy that car.
    A payment   **B** salary   **C** wages   **D** money

8   I am writing to complain about a recent problem I had with a member of your ....
    A company   **B** employees   **C** staff   **D** workplace

9   The company lost a great deal of money when one of their .... was found to be faulty.
    A goods   **B** products   **C** manufacture   **D** business

10 The government should do more to help the .... find a job.
    A employed   **B** employment   **C** unemployment   **D** unemployed

11 Taking a packed lunch to work can be a lot more .... than buying it every day.
    A economical   **B** economics   **C** expenditure   **D** expenses

12 I'd really like to find a .... during the summer holidays.
    A job   **B** work   **C** profession   **D** career

13 I think that people who .... serious crimes should be punished.
    A convict   **B** commit   **C** offend   **D** offence

14 I had to pay a .... for parking my car in a restricted area.
    A fine   **B** find   **C** fee   **D** form

15 Helping poor people to find a job may help to .... crime.
   A avoid   **B** deter   **C** impose   **D** prevent

16 I don't agree with .... very young or petty criminals.
   A committing   **B** enforcing   **C** imprisoning   **D** offending

17 In most countries, it is .... the law to steal other people's property.
   A against   **B** by   **C** for   **D** with

18 The government should .... a law to make computer hacking illegal.
   A abolish   **B** bring   **C** enter   **D** pass

19 I don't like this newspaper, the reports are really .... towards the government.
   A biased   **B** prejudiced   **C** reliable   **D** well-informed

20 Tabloid newspapers are a good example of .... media.
   A masses   **B** mass   **C** main   **D** multi

21 I think following celebrities on their holidays is an .... of privacy.
   A avoidance   **B** invasive   **C** intrusion   **D** invasion

22 The popular press often contains a lot more .... than hard facts.
   A speculation   **B** realism   **C** influence   **D** tolerance

23 When celebrities behave badly it can have a negative influence .... young people.
   A for   **B** in   **C** on   **D** to

24 I enjoy learning about celebrities in magazines and .... TV.
   A by   **B** from   **C** in   **D** on

25 I think successful writers and artists are very ....
   A imaginative   **B** imagination   **C** inspiration   **D** inspire

26 This artist helps to preserve our local .... by using traditional themes in his work.
   A culture   **B** creation   **C** events   **D** skills

27 I don't really appreciate classical music, I prefer the .... arts such as painting and sculpture.
   A festival   **B** literary   **C** performing   **D** visual

28 The .... enjoyed the performance so much that they gave a 10-minute standing ovation.
   A artists   **B** audience   **C** players   **D** participants

29 My friends and I have the same .... in music.
   A type   **B** topic   **C** theme   **D** taste

30 I was so embarrassed when my teacher made me .... my song in front of the whole school.
   A participate   **B** participant   **C** perform   **D** performance

21 Language building 1
Using a dictionary, word families

Using a dictionary

1.1 Answer these questions about your dictionary.

1 What type of dictionary do you have?
   A English → English   B English → your language   C Your language → English

2 When do you use it?
   A Only in class.   B Only at home.   C At home and in class.

3 Which of the following is true for you?
   A I look up every word I don't know.
   B I only use my dictionary to check words after I have done an exercise.
   C I've got a dictionary, but I rarely use it.

> ### Study Tip
>
> There are several different types of dictionary. Make sure you are familiar with yours and the way it is organised. Try to use a monolingual dictionary as this will help you to practise your English more. If you are using a small pocket or electronic dictionary you may find that it does not contain many of the words you need to look up and it will not give you example sentences. If you would like to buy a dictionary, Exercises 1.3 and 1.4 might help you to assess the different dictionaries you find. Don't use your dictionary to look up every new word. When you are using this book use the context to work out the meaning of a word and then complete the exercises. Use your dictionary when you have finished. When you are writing, use your dictionary to help with spellings as well as the correct usage of a word.

1.2 The words in column A are all related to dictionaries. Match the words to the correct meaning in column B.

A		B	
1	monolingual	A	a large amount of written material organised to show how language works
2	bilingual	B	written in only one language
3	corpus	C	a word that means the same
4	synonym	D	a dictionary containing synonyms and antonyms
5	antonym	E	the sound and pronunciation of words
6	thesaurus	F	written in two different languages for translation purposes
7	phonology	G	the origin of words
8	etymology	H	a word that means the opposite

1.3 Do you know how your dictionary is organised?

1 How can you tell whether the word is a noun/verb/adjective etc.?

2 How does it tell you the pronunciation of the word?

3 Does it give you other words in the same family?

4 Does it give you example sentences?

5 Does it tell you whether a word is slang or taboo?

6 Does it tell you which other words can / need to be used with this word?

7 What information is given in the front of your dictionary? Does it give:
   • information about measurements?
   • information about grammar?
   • hints on how to use the dictionary?
   • an explanation of the phonetic script used?
   • a list of abbreviations used?

> ### Study Tip
>
> If you look up a verb in your dictionary, you should see the following in brackets after it: *vt* or *vi* (sometimes simply *t* or *i*). This tells you whether the verb is *transitive* or *intransitive*. A transitive verb needs, or can have, an object, e.g. *put: I **put** the vase on the table. Put* is transitive because it must have an object (the vase). NOT *I put on the table*.
> An *intransitive* verb does not need, or cannot have, an object, e.g. *rise: The sun **rises** every morning. Rise* is intransitive because it has no object. Not *I rise the table*. Some verbs can be transitive or intransitive, e.g. *carry: I **carried** the table to another room.* (Transitive, the object = *the table*.); *His voice **carried** across the room.* (Intransitive, his voice didn't carry anything.)

1.4 Look up the words *evolve, exist, develop* and *swerve* in your dictionary and then answer these questions.

1 Which verb(s) are transitive and which are intransitive? ....

2 Which verb(s) can be either? ....

3 Which verb(s) can have an object and which verb(s) cannot have an object? ....

4 Which verb(s) means the same as:
   A move uncontrollably ....   B be ....
   C change or grow? ....

5 Does the verb *swerve* rhyme with   A curve   B halve   C mauve? ....

1.5 Abbreviations are often used in a dictionary to give you information about words. What do the following abbreviations stand for? Choose a word from the box that you might find these abbreviations next to.

1 adj ......*= adjective: good*......   choice   of   good   well   kids   differ

2 n ....

3 vi ....

4 sl ....

5 adv ....

6 prep ....

1.6 Some words can have more than one meaning so don't assume the first reference you find is the meaning you are looking for. Match the words in column A to two possible meanings in column B. Use a dictionary to help you if necessary.

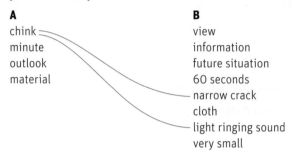

A	B
chink	view
minute	information
outlook	future situation
material	60 seconds
	narrow crack
	cloth
	light ringing sound
	very small

1.7 (🎧 21) A dictionary can also help you to pronounce words correctly using phonetic symbols. Listen to the recording and then match the vowel sounds that are underlined with the correct phonetic symbol.

put   th**e**se   **i**n   s**o**me   b**a**ll   ch**oo**se   w**o**rd   **a**bout   g**ue**st   wh**a**t   att**a**ck   h**a**rd

Phonetic symbols

iː these	uː	ɜː	ɑː	ɔː	e
ɒ	ʌ	æ	ə	ʊ	ɪ

Study Tip

A good dictionary will also tell you which other words can or need to be used with the word you are checking. This is called *collocation*. Collocation will help you to use new words accurately in a sentence. When you look up a new word in your dictionary, make a note of the words that collocate with it. The example sentences can help with this.

Study the following extract from the *Cambridge Advanced Learner's Dictionary*. You will see that the word *choice* can be used in several different ways and have a variety of collocations.

WORDS THAT GO WITH *choice* [ACT]

have a choice • make a choice • give/offer sb a choice • be faced with a choice • an informed choice • a choice between [two things or people] • a choice of sth • by/from choice

choice [ACT] ❸ /tʃɔɪs/ *noun* [C or U] an act or the possibility of choosing: *If the product doesn't work, you are given the choice of a refund or a replacement.* ○ *It's a difficult choice to* **make**. ○ *It's your choice/The choice is yours* (= only you can decide). ○ *It was a choice* **between** *pain now or pain later, so I chose pain later.* ○ *Now you know all the facts, you can make an* **informed** *choice.* ○ *I'd prefer not to work but I don't* **have much** *choice* (= this is not possible). ○ *He* **had no** *choice* **but** *to accept* (= He had to accept). ○ *Is she single* **by** *choice?*

WORDS THAT GO WITH *choice* [VARIETY]

a bewildering/excellent/wide choice • offer a choice of sth • a choice of sth

choice [VARIETY] ❶ /tʃɔɪs/ *noun* [S or U] the range of different things from which you can choose: *There wasn't much choice on the menu.* ○ *The evening menu offers a* **wide** *choice of dishes.* ○ *The dress is available* **in** *a choice of colours.*

Word families

V *Vocabulary note*

A prefix is a letter, or group of letters, that can be added to the beginning of a word to make a new word. Prefixes can help you to work out the meaning of unknown words. The prefix *re* means to do again, e.g. *use*, **re***use* = to use again. A suffix is a letter, or group of letters, that can be added to the end of a word to form a new word. The suffix *able* means it is possible to do something, e.g. *assess*, *assess**able*** (= it is possible to assess). In your dictionary, a prefix will be shown with a hyphen after it (*re-*); a suffix will be shown with a hyphen in front of it (*-able*).

2.1 Use your dictionary to check other words that can be made from the same base word. Put the following words into the correct columns to make new words.

approach assess assume create define distribute establish identify interpret represent vary

-ment	-tion	-able	mis-	re-	un-
....	....	....	....	....	....
....	....	....	....	....	....
....	....	....	....	....	....
....	....	....	....	....	....
....	....	....	....	....	....
....	....	....	....	....	....
....	....	....	....	....	....
....	....	....	....	....	....

2.2 Consider the longest word in the English language: *antidisestablishmentarianism*. Base form = *establish* (+ *-ment*) = *establishment* (+ *dis-*) = *disestablishment* (+ *-arian*) = *disestablishmentarian* (+ *-ism*) = *disestablishmentarianism* (+ *anti-*) = *antidisestablishmentarianism*.

Which of the groups of letters in column A are prefixes and which are suffixes? Match them to the meanings in column B.

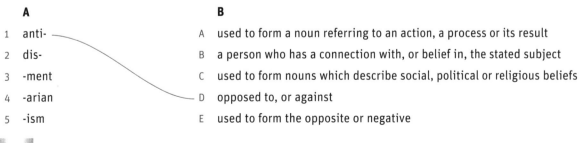

A

1 anti-

2 dis-

3 -ment

4 -arian

5 -ism

B

A used to form a noun referring to an action, a process or its result

B a person who has a connection with, or belief in, the stated subject

C used to form nouns which describe social, political or religious beliefs

D opposed to, or against

E used to form the opposite or negative

2.3 Think of an example word for each of the prefixes and suffixes in column A above.

22 Language building 2
Learning vocabulary, collocation

Learning vocabulary

1.1 Create a list.

Each week, try to build up a list of new words you have seen or read. These may be words you are familiar with, but don't know well enough to use actively or accurately. Don't make the list too long – ten should be enough. Here are ten useful words for this week.

1 analysis
2 benefit
3 consistent
4 create
5 define

6 environment
7 occur
8 period
9 significant
10 theory

1.2 Check the meaning.

Make sure you understand the meaning of each of the words in **1.1**. Which of them is closest in meaning to each of the following?

A happen ....

B make ....

C reliable ....

D close examination ....

E important ....

F length of time ....

G advantage ....

H opinion or explanation ....

I clearly show ....

J surroundings ....

1.3 Find out the different forms of each word.

1 Look again at the words 1–10 in **1.1**. Write *N* next to the nouns, *V* next to the verbs and *A* next to the adjectives.

2 Which word can be a noun or a verb? ....

3 Which of the words can have the following prefixes: *in*, *re*?

1.4 WORD BUILDING Complete the table with the different forms of each of the words in 1.1.

	Noun	Verb	Adjective		Noun	Verb	Adjective
1				6			
2				7			
3				8			
4				9			
5				10			

1.5 Learn how to pronounce the words.

1 **22a** Listen and practise saying each word.

2 **22b** Now listen to ten sentences (a–j). Each contains a word from **1.1**, but in a different form. Write down each word and its form (noun, verb etc.).

A *environmentalist (noun)* ....

B ....

C ....

D ....

E ....

F ....

G ....

H ....

I ....

J ....

3 **22b** Now listen to the sentences again and mark the stress on each of the words you have written. Practise saying the sentences.

> ### Study Tip
>
> When you are learning new words, look carefully to see if there are any spelling rules that can help you. Make a note of any double letters. It is sometimes easier to break the longer words up, e.g. *en-vi-ron-ment*.

1.6 Know how to spell the words.

Study the spellings of words 1–10 in **1.1**, then cover up the words. Now underline the correct spellings below.

1 analasis   <u>analysis</u>   analisis

2 beneficial   benefitial   benefisial

3 consistent   consistant   concistent

4 recretion   recreation   recration

5 defined   defind   defende

6 enviroment   environment   environement

7 occurred   ocurred   ocured

8 periodicaly   periodicly   periodically

9 sinificant   singnificant   significant

10 theoretical   theretical   theorretical

1.7 Use the words.

Complete this text with the correct form of the words in 1.1.

> ### Study Tip
>
> Try to use new words as often as possible when speaking and writing. They should start to become part of your active vocabulary. Look back at new words as often as you can and test yourself on the meaning, pronunciation and spelling.

Nowadays we hear the word 'sustainable' being used a great deal in academic journals and [1] ...... *periodicals* .... [2] .... in particular are very concerned that any development should be 'sustainable'. They argue that sustainable practices have great [3] .... for us and can have a [4] .... impact on the future of our planet.

However, the word 'sustainable' needs to be clearly [5] .... Sustainable development [6] .... in exploiting our natural resources without destroying them. We need to establish whether this can be put into practice or whether it is a mere [7] .... There needs to be a thorough [8] .... of any development plans before they are allowed to proceed, as once an area has been destroyed it is almost impossible to [9] .... it. We should do our best to ensure that there is no [10] .... of the logging and land clearing that destroyed so many forests at the start of the twentieth century.

1.8 🎧 **22b** **Remember the context.**

Look at the following ideas or contexts, which were all used in the sentences in **1.4**. Which words from **1.4** do you associate them with? Listen again to check your answers.

1   very bad storms ....*occurred*........

2   global warming ....

3   the student council ....

4   growing plants ....

5   eating fish ....

6   studying chemistry ....

7   video games and violence ....

8   space exploration and Mars ....

9   a teacher commenting on an essay ....

10   young children and the impact of school ....

1.9   **Use spelling rules to help you edit your work.**

1   Change these words by adding the endings in brackets.

A   surprise ....*surprising*........ (*ing*)

B   true .... (*ly*)

C   advance .... (*ment*)

D   happy .... (*est*)

E   worry .... (*ed*)

F   worry .... (*ing*)

G   unplug .... (*ed*)

H   stop .... (*ed*)

I   slope .... (*ed*)

J   change .... (*able*)

2   Add an appropriate prefix (*dis*, *im*, *in* or *un*) to these words.

A   suitable ....*unsuitable*........

B   appropriate ....

C   similar ....

D   noticed ....

E   interested ....

F   patient ....

G   ability ....

H   organised ....

I   polite ....

J   employment ....

Collocation

2.1   **Learn important collocations. Correct the collocation errors in these sentences.**

1   After a careful analysis from the situation we decided to cancel the trip.

   ....

2   Regular exercise can be to benefit for people with asthma.

   ....

3   These results are consistent to the ones we obtained last month.

   ....

4   We need to create for a new design.

   ....

5 I am looking up the definition from this word.

....

6 We should use products that are environmentally good.

....

2.2 Complete the sentences with the correct prepositions from the box.

1 The president refused to comment .... the problem.

2 I found out about the hotel .... the Internet.

about   for   in   on   to   with   of

3 I would like to apply .... the position of head chef.

4 The students were allowed .... participate .... the basketball tournament.

5 I was completely satisfied .... the service at your hotel.

6 My mother is concerned .... the amount .... money I spend each week.

7 The cost .... living has increased by 5 per cent this year.

8 There are several reasons .... this increase.

2.3 Which word in each list cannot collocate with the word in bold?

1 difficulty / ~~knowledge~~ / need / opportunity / problem   **arise**

2 draw / have / need / pay / receive / seek   **attention**

3 assess / cause / inflict / repair / take   **damage**

4 attract / develop / excite / feign / give / lose   **interest**

5 acquire / learn / speak / tell / use   **language**

6 control / an exam / a law / judgment / the time   **pass**

 Vocabulary note

When using an adverb with an adjective, note the following:

extremely = 'to a large degree' so it should not be used with adjectives that have an extreme meaning, e.g. *terrified*. You need to use a neutral adverb, e.g. *completely, really: completely terrified*. NOT ~~extremely terrified~~.

slightly = 'to a small degree', so cannot be used with extreme adjectives: *slightly scared*. NOT ~~slightly terrified~~.

significantly is often used with comparative adjectives: *significantly greater*. NOT ~~significantly great~~.

Other collocations just have to be learned.

2.4 Choose the correct adverb in each sentence.

1 I was *completely* / *utterly* satisfied with my test result.

2 It is highly *likely* / *possible* that the president will resign today.

3 The machine was *slightly* / *utterly* useless.

4 I am *extremely* / *totally* concerned about your behaviour.

5 It was *bitterly* / *completely* cold in the winter.

6 I was *absolutely* / *totally* freezing by the time we arrived.

7 The oil spill had a *big* / *heavy* impact on the surrounding environment.

8 It is *absolutely* / *very* impossible to predict the future with any certainty.

Study Tip

Once you have done all of these things, you should be able to say that you *know* a word.

Data, graphs and tables

1.1 Match the labels to the correct illustrations.

1 pie chart   2 table   3 bar chart / bar graph   4 graph   5 diagram   6 flowchart

A
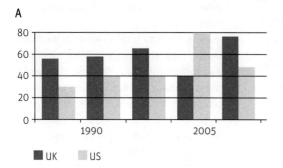

B

1.	collect rubbish
2.	sort
3.	wash glass bottles
4.	crush

C
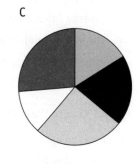

D
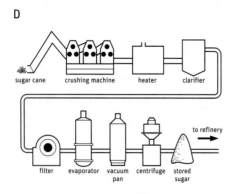

E

F

Sydney	3.6
Melbourne	2.9
Brisbane	2.6
Canberra	1.8

1.2 Look at this writing task. Which data do you think is the most significant?

You should spend about 20 minutes on this task.

Write a report for a university lecturer describing the information below.

Write at least 150 words.

The graph below shows how much waste is collected and recycled in the US.

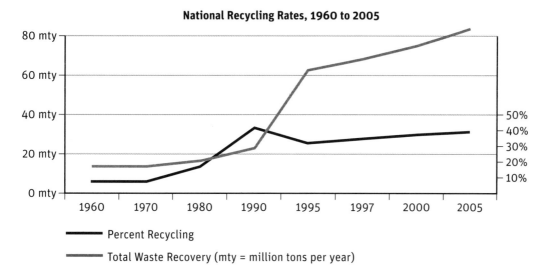

National Recycling Rates, 1960 to 2005

Percent Recycling

Total Waste Recovery (mty = million tons per year)

1.3 Which two of the following sentences do NOT refer to significant information on the graph?

1 The amount of waste being recycled rose from 30% to 32% between 2000 and 2005.

2 The amount of waste material being recycled reached a peak in 1990.

3 The amount of garbage being collected annually rose from approximately 10 million tonnes to 55 million tonnes between 1990 and 1995.

4 The amount of garbage being produced each year rose from 5.6 to 8 million tonnes between 1960 and 1970.

5 The percentage of rubbish being recycled rose from 6.8% to 33.2% between 1970 and 1990.

1.4 Put these words and phrases into the correct column according to the trend they can be used to describe. Some of the words can be used to describe more than one pattern.

unchanged	fall	rise	drop	remain steady	reach a high
fluctuate	plunge	upward trend	downward trend	plateau	sharp
steep	unpredictable	static	significant	wildly	constant
reach a low	steadily	rapidly	fixed	peak	

↘	↗	→	↘ ↗ ↘ ↗
fall	rise	unchanged	fluctuate

1.5 Correct the preposition mistakes in these sentences. You will need to refer to the writing task in **1.2**.

1 The amount of garbage being recycled rose ~~by~~ 32% between 1995 and 2005. ....*to*........

2 The amount of garbage being recycled rose significantly in 1970 and 1990. ....

3 The percentage of garbage being recycled rose from 3% between 1970 and 1980. ....

4 The amount of garbage being produced rose to 16.2 million tonnes between 1995 and 2005. ....

1.6 Change the sentences below from *adjective + noun* to *verb + adverb*, or vice versa. Use your notebook.

1 There was a significant increase in the number of birds in 1994.

2 The number of people attending fell considerably in 2002.

3 The percentage of female students rose dramatically in 1990.

4 There was a noticeable drop in temperatures between 1880 and 1885.

5 The figures changed constantly between 2001 and 2006.

6 There was a slight increase in temperatures in 1909.

Error warning!

When comparing statistics we usually say: **Comparing** *the figures for 1999 and 2000, we can see an increase of 20%.* NOT ~~Compared the figures for 1999.~~ We use **compared to** or **compared with** as follows: **Compared to** *the number of males, the number of females is relatively low.* NOT ~~Comparing with the number of females.~~ Or: *The number of males is quite large* **compared to/with** *the number of females.* NOT ~~comparing to the number of ...~~

Vocabulary note

Note the way we use prepositions with numbers and dates:

35%	10%
1995	1997

In 1997 the number fell **to** *10%;* **In** *1997 the number fell* **by** *25%;* **In** *1997 the number fell* **from** *35%.* NOT ~~in 35%;~~ *The number dropped* **to** *10%* **between** *1995 and 1997.* NOT ~~reduced to;~~ **By** *1997 the number had fallen* **to** *10%.* See also units 7 and 13.

Vocabulary note

You can use a combination of verb + adverb, or adjective + noun, to avoid repeating the same phrases and to add extra meaning: *There was a* **significant increase** *in the numbers. The numbers* **increased significantly**. Notice that you need a preposition when you use the noun form: *There was an* **increase in** *attendance; There was a* **drop of** *10%.* NOT ~~There was an increase attendance. There was a drop 10%.~~

1.7 Complete the description of the graph in **1.2** with the correct form of the words in the box. Some words can be used more than once.

between	static	compare	rise	peak
dramatic	from	to	increase	steady
	fall	in	gradual	by	

The graph shows the amount of garbage collected and recycled annually in America [1]........*between*........ 1960 and 2005. From 1960 to 1970 the amount of waste being recycled remained fairly [2].......................... at just over 6%. However, this figure [3].......................... significantly from 1970 to 1990 when it [4].......................... at approximately 32% of the total waste collected. On the other hand, the amount of waste being produced increased [5].......................... at around the same time, growing [6].......................... approximately 10 million tonnes per year [7].......................... 55 million tonnes within five years. Following this sharp [8].......................... the amount of waste collected has risen [9].......................... , while the percentage of waste being recycled actually [10].......................... from 32% to 26% [11].......................... 1995. Fortunately, recycling has [12].......................... increased and [13].......................... 2005 it had again reached the same figure as in 1990. However, this figure is still disappointing [14].......................... to the total amount of waste that is thrown away.

Describing a diagram or a process

2.1 Look at the following diagram and answer the questions.

1   At what stage is something added?

2   At what stage is something separated?

3   How many different stages are there altogether?

How chewing gum is made

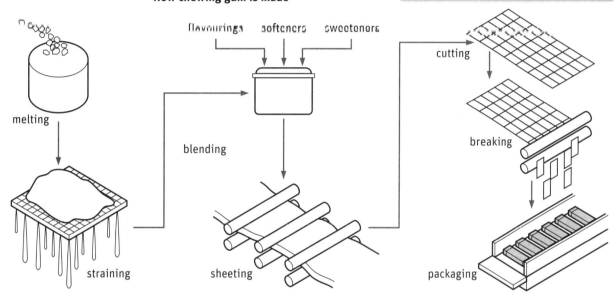

2.2 Now complete the description of the diagram with the correct form of the words in the box. You will need to use some of the words more than once.

add	container	first	finally	heat	ingredients	liquid	machine
mixture	next	pass	pieces	place	shapes	show	then	travel

The diagram (1)......*shows*.............. how chewing gum is produced. (2)............................ the (3)............................ of gum are put into a (4)............................ and (5)............................ until they form a single mass . This is (6)............................ strained until all of the (7)............................ has been eliminated. (8)............................ , the gum is (9)............................ into another (10)............................ and the desired flavourings, sweeteners and softeners are (11)............................ . This (12)............................ is blended until all of the (13)............................ are mixed together. The gum then (14)............................ to a different (15)............................ which uses rollers to flatten out the gum. (16)........................., the thin sheets of gum are cut into rectangular (17)............................ and broken into separate (18)............................ . (19)............................, the gum (20)............................ along a conveyor belt where it is enclosed in packaging ready for distribution .

24 Academic Writing Task 2
Linking words, opinion words, register

Getting started

1.1 Look at this essay question and consider whether you agree or disagree with the statement.

> A lot of students find it difficult to write good essays. There is little that you can do to make your essays better or to make the job easier.

> To what extent do you agree or disagree?

1.2 Replace the underlined words in the introductory sentences below with a suitable word from the box.

| task | less difficult | struggle | produce | high-quality | many | improve |

> It is true that <u>a lot of</u> students <u>find it difficult</u> to <u>write</u> <u>good</u> essays. I don't agree that there is little you can do to <u>make</u> your essays <u>better</u> or to make the <u>job easier.</u>

Linking words

2.1 These words and phrases can be used to link ideas together. Put the words and phrases into the correct column according to their function. Use your notebook.

similarly	that is	now
as a result	alternatively	in other words
indeed	and	consequently
nonetheless	while	to illustrate this
finally	whereas	firstly
however	in conclusion	therefore
although	but	because
secondly	because of	or
despite	not only … but … also…	also
in addition	furthermore	on the other hand
such as	to summarise	for example

> **Vocabulary note**
>
> *Because* is a conjuction and is used to give a reason: *The car crashed **because** the brakes didn't work.* *Because of* is a preposition and means *as a result of*: *The hospital closed **because of** a lack of funds.*

Sequencing ideas	Adding supporting ideas	Introducing a contrasting idea	Giving examples	Giving an alternative	Giving an explanation	Drawing a conclusion
firstly						

Test Tip

Support your ideas with evidence and relevant examples. Make sure that your ideas are well organised and easy to follow by using the correct linking words.

2.2 **Underline the correct linking words in the following sentences.**

1 It can be difficult to write an essay, *because / although* there are several things you can do to make the job easier.

2 There are several things you can do to make writing easier. *For example / However*, it can be helpful to make a rough plan of your ideas.

3 It can be helpful to practise writing within the time limit. You can time yourself with a clock *and / or* a stopwatch.

4 You will not be allowed to use equipment *as a result / such as* a dictionary during the test.

5 I think I did well in the test *although / in spite of* I did run out of time at the end.

6 I think that my vocabulary has improved *because / as a result of* reading this book.

 Vocabulary note

The following linking words and phrases must be followed by a noun and cannot be followed by a clause: *because of, as a result of, in spite of, despite: I enjoyed my holiday **in spite of** the bad weather.* NOT *in spite of the weather was bad.*

2.3 **Improve the essay by inserting the correct linking words and phrases. There may be more than one possible answer.**

however	firstly	in other words	furthermore	also	such as
alternatively	now	nevertheless	in addition	because	similarly

It is true that many students struggle to produce high-quality essays. (1) <u>However / Nevertheless</u> I don't agree that there is little you can do to improve your essays or to make the task less difficult.

(2) ...., let us examine what an essay needs in order to be considered 'good'. To begin with, a good essay must answer the question fully. (3) .... it must address each of the points raised in the essay title. (4) ...., it must present these points in an organised and logical way. A good writer will (5) .... avoid using the same words and phrases. This can be easily achieved by using techniques (6) .... paraphrasing. (7) ...., you can use synonyms of words rather than repeating the same ones. (8) ...., all of the ideas presented in your essay must be relevant and supported by examples.

(9) ...., let us consider what students can do in order to improve their essay-writing skills. Clearly, a good knowledge of the language is required to be able to write an essay that has few errors and communicates well. (10) ...., writing a good essay requires more than good language skills (11) .... people often find it difficult to write essays even in their own language. As with any skill, the best way to learn is from our mistakes. To learn how to ride a bike you need to get on one and fall off a few times. (12) ...., students can improve their essay writing through making and correcting mistakes and through constant practice.

Opinion words

 Vocabulary note

We often use adverbs to show our opinion of an idea.

3.1 Match the adverbs in column A with the correct meaning in column B.

A		B	
1	personally	A	it is easy to understand
2	unfortunately	B	it is easy to understand
3	clearly	C	it is well deserved
4	obviously	D	this is my own opinion
5	justifiably	E	I believe this is a sad thing
6	thankfully	F	I believe this is a good thing
7	fortunately	G	I believe this is a good thing

Error warning!

Be careful with punctuation. You must use a comma after the following words
and phrases when they are used at the start of a sentence: *In addition, Also,
For example, In conclusion, Finally, However, Furthermore, Lastly, In my opinion,
Similarly, To summarise, Therefore, Unfortunately, To sum up*, e.g. *To sum up, in my
opinion taking a gap year is a very good idea.* NOT ~~To sum up in my opinion...~~

3.2 Complete the sentences with adverbs from **3.1**. Don't forget the necessary punctuation.

1 ....*Personally*........, I think learning vocabulary is a good idea.

2 .... I remembered how to spell the word correctly on the day of the exam.

3 When I received my results I was .... proud.

4 .... my friend didn't study for the test so he didn't do very well.

5 .... if you work hard then you will improve.

Finishing off and register

Test Tip

Use your conclusion to summarise your main points. When you have finished,
carefully edit your work and check your spelling.

4.1 It is easy to make careless spelling mistakes if you are writing quickly. Read the following paragraph and correct the spelling mistakes.

Recnet resaerch at an Engilsh uinervtisy sugegsts taht it deosn't mttaer waht oredr the ltteers in a wrod are, the olny impotarnt tihng is that the frist and lsat ltteers are in the rghit pclae. Eevn thuogh the mddile ltteers mghit be mxied up, people dno't hvae a prolbem raeding the wrods. Tihs is becuase we raed the wrod as a wohle rahter tahn eevry ltteer by iteslf.

> **Test Tip**
>
> *Slang* = very informal, *taboo* = this word will offend people. The IELTS test is a formal situation, so you should never use informal words, e.g. ~~kids, guys~~. You should also avoid using abbreviations: **number** NOT ~~no.~~ , **for example** NOT ~~e.g.~~ , you and your NOT ~~U/UR~~.

4.2 Correct the mistakes with register and spelling that have been underlined in the conclusion. Which words do you have to change because of register?

To sum up, even [1] through many [2]guys think writing essays is [3]a bit difficult, there [4]is stuff they can do to [5]imporve [6]there writing skills. [7]Personaly, I [8]belive that if you [9]wanna get a good score in an exam situation then you need to make sure that you [10]aproach the essay question in a logical and organised way. Finally, you need [11]too leave enough time to check over your work [12]throughly at the end.

1 .... *though* ....

2 ....

3 ....

4 ....

5 ....

6 ....

7 ....

8 ....

9 ....

10 ....

11 ....

12 ....

25 General Training Writing

Vocabulary for Writing Tasks 1 and 2

Writing Task 1

1.1 Put the words into the correct column according to the type of letter they might be used in. Use your notebook.

apologise	applicant	appreciate	forgive
attend	be considered	excuse	invitation
confirm	dissatisfied	interview	would be
grateful	help	suggest	delighted
propose	sorry	ask	
unhappy	wonder	complain	

Test Tip

General Training Writing Task 1 is always a letter. You will be given a problem or a situation and you have to write a letter in response to this. Don't copy the words from the question paper – use your own words. You must address all of the points raised and make sure that your ideas are organised in a logical way. When you have finished, check your spelling and that you have written at least 150 words. Remember to leave enough time for Task 2!

Acceptance	Application	Apology	Complaint	Enquiry	Recommendation	Thanks
would be delighted						

1.2 Use a word from the table in **1.1** to complete the sentences.

1 I am writing to ....*apologise*........ for my behaviour last night. It was inexcusable.

2 I would like to .... about the treatment I received at your hotel.

3 I hope that you will .... me for behaving in this way.

4 I am very .... for the amount of time you have given up to help me.

5 Unfortunately, I will not be able to .... the party.

6 I am writing to .... for your help in finding a place to live.

1.3 Underline the correct preposition in each sentence. Sometimes no preposition is necessary.

1 I am sorry _for_ / _from_ the damage that I caused.

2 The manager told – / _to_ me that there were no rooms available.

3 I was unhappy _for_ / _with_ the way I was treated by your staff.

4 I would like to enquire _about_ / _for_ renting a car.

5 I would like to be considered _in_ / _for_ the position advertised.

6 I am available to attend – / _to_ an interview at any time.

7 I would like to explain – / _of_ what happened.

8 Would you be able to help – / _to_ me?

9 Thank you _about_ / _for_ all of the help you have given me.

10 I am looking forward _for_ / _to_ seeing you soon.

Vocabulary note

Note that the phrasal verb _to look forward_ is always followed by _to + ing_: _I am **looking forward to** catching up with you soon._ In formal letters we use the simple present tense rather than the present continuous: _I **look** forward to hearing from you in the near future._

1.4 Match the words in column A with the words in column B to form some common phrases used at the end of letters.

A

Thank you
I would be
I look
I have enclosed
Best
Kind
Yours
Yours

B

my CV
faithfully
in advance
sincerely
regards
grateful if you could
wishes
forward to

Vocabulary note

Be careful with the spelling of the following words: *grateful*, *sincerely*, *faithfully*. Register is important when writing a letter. Make sure the language you use is not too informal if the letter is a very formal one, or too formal if the letter is to someone you know well.

1.5 What is the best way to begin and end a letter to these people?

1 a friend, or someone you know well and address by their first name

2 your employer

3 a person you have never met

4 a person you have met only briefly, but whose name you know

Writing Task 2

2.1 Look at the following essay question and decide whether you agree or disagree with the statement in bold.

You should spend about 40 minutes on this task.

Write about the following topic.

A lot of people find it difficult to write letters and often avoid doing so altogether. Letter writing is a dying art.

Do you agree with this statement?

Give reasons for your answer and include any relevant examples.

Write at least 250 words.

Test Tip

Writing Task 2 is a discursive essay. You will be given a topic to write about. You should write a plan so that your ideas are organised logically and coherently. Try to use a wide variety of vocabulary and don't copy words from the question paper. Try not to repeat the same words or ideas. When you have finished, check your spelling and make sure you have written at least 250 words.

2.2 Replace the underlined words in the introductory sentences below with a suitable word or phrase from the box.

writing letters   gradually disappearing   struggle   produce
this skill   many   frequently   completely

It is true that <u>a lot of</u> people <u>find it difficult</u> to <u>write</u> letters and <u>often</u> avoid <u>doing so altogether</u>. I don't agree that <u>letter writing</u> is <u>a dying art</u>.

Linking words

3.1 These words and phrases can be used to link ideas together. Put the words and phrases into the correct column according to their function. Use your notebook.

similarly	in addition	but	first
as a result	such as	because of	therefore
nonetheless	that is	not only ... but ... also...	because
finally	alternatively	furthermore	or
however	and	to summarise	also
although	while	now	on the other hand
secondly	whereas	in other words	for example
despite	in conclusion	consequently	

Sequencing ideas	Adding supporting ideas	Introducing a contrasting idea	Giving examples	Giving an alternative	Giving an explanation	Drawing a conclusion
First						

3.2 Underline the correct linking word in the following sentences.

1 It can be difficult to write an essay, *because / <u>although</u>* there are several things you can do to make the job easier.

2 There are several things you can do to make writing easier. *For example / However*, it can be helpful to make a rough plan of your ideas.

3 It can be helpful to practise writing within the time limit. You can time yourself with a clock *and / or* a stopwatch.

4 You will not be allowed to use equipment *as a result / such as* a dictionary during the test.

5 I think I did well in the test *although / in spite of* I did run out of time at the end.

6 I think that my vocabulary has improved *because / as a result of* reading this book.

> ### Vocabulary note
> The following linking words and phrases must be followed by a noun and not a clause: *because of, as a result of, in spite of, despite*: *I enjoyed my holiday **in spite of** the bad weather.* NOT ~~in spite of the weather was bad.~~

3.3 Improve the essay by inserting the correct linking words and phrases. There may be more than one possible answer.

however   firstly   furthermore   such as   nevertheless   in addition   consequently   because
particularly   because of   as a result

It is true that many people struggle to produce letters and often avoid writing letters completely.
(1) <u>However / Nevertheless</u>, I don't agree that this skill is gradually disappearing.

(2) ...., let us consider the reasons why people find it so difficult to write. To begin with, writing letters is less frequent nowadays thanks to modern technology. These days we are much more likely to email someone than write a letter. (3) ...., our business communications have become more informal than in the past. (4) .... a less formal style of writing is more acceptable. Other forms of modern communication (5) .... text messaging have reduced our writing skills even further.

(6) .... I still feel that letter writing is an important skill to learn (7) .... there are many parts of the world where it is very important to be formal. This is (8) .... true if you are involved in international business. (9) .... globalisation, the business world is becoming more and more international and it is not always possible to pick up the telephone to talk to people. (10) ...., I believe that letter writing will never die out completely. And, even though these letters may be written on computers rather than by hand, we still need to learn and practise this skill.

Opinion words

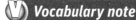 **Vocabulary note**

> We often use adverbs to show our opinion of an idea.

4.1 Match the adverbs in column A with the correct meaning in column B.

	A		B
1	personally	A	it is easy to understand
2	unfortunately	B	it is easy to understand
3	clearly	C	it is well deserved
4	obviously	D	this is my own opinion
5	justifiably	E	I believe this is a sad thing
6	thankfully	F	I believe this is a good thing
7	fortunately	G	I believe this is a good thing

4.2 Complete the sentences with adverbs from 4.1.

1 ....*Personally*........, I think learning vocabulary is a good idea.

2 ...., I remembered how to spell the word correctly on the day of the exam.

3 He worked very hard, so when he received his test results he was .... proud.

4 ...., my friend didn't study for the test so he didn't do very well.

5 ...., if you work hard then you will improve.

Finishing off and register

5 Correct the mistakes with register and spelling that have been underlined in the conclusion. Which words do you have to change because of register?

Test Tip

In formal essay writing you must use the correct register. This means you should avoid using informal words e.g. ~~kids, guys~~. You should also avoid using abbreviations and write out the words in full: **number** NOT ~~no.~~, **for example** NOT ~~e.g.~~

To sum up, even ¹through many ²guys think writing letters is ³a bit difficult, there ⁴is stuff they can do to ⁵imporve ⁶there writing skills if they find it ⁷to difficult. ⁸Personaly, I ⁹belive that if you ¹⁰wanna make a good ¹¹impresion in any situation, then you need good ¹²writting skills.

1	....*though*....	5	....	9	....
2	....	6	....	10	....
3	....	7	....	11	....
4	....	8	....	12	....

Test Five (Units 21–25)

Choose the correct letter A, B, C or D.

1 John .... on the table and called for everyone's attention.
   A held   **B** placed   **C** put   **D** stood

2 We have decided to .... a new industrial zone to encourage more businesses to move into the area.
   A evolve   **B** grow up   **C** develop   **D** exist

3 The word *put* rhymes with ....
   A suit   **B** cut   **C** foot   **D** blood

4 I never met our old school principal, but the new one seems very ....
   A approachment   **B** approachable   **C** misapproach   **D** unapproach

5 We don't encourage .... social behaviour such as vandalism.
   A anti-   **B** dis   **C** pre   **D** un

6 The word *organise* is a .... of the word *arrange*.
   A antonym   **B** corpus   **C** collocation   **D** synonym

7 There are other books on this topic but Smith's is thought to be the .... work.
   A definite   **B** definition   **C** definitive   **D** define

8 .... many elderly people struggle to meet their everyday living expenses.
   A Now days   **B** Nowday   **C** Nowdays   **D** Nowadays

9 You need to choose a new assignment topic – this one is not .... to the one you chose last term.
   A dissimilar   **B** insimilar   **C** nonsimilar   **D** unsimilar

10 There are several reasons .... this change in decision.
   A by   **B** for   **C** of   **D** why

11 The lecturer .... our attention to a large screen at the back of the room.
   A drew   **B** pointed   **C** gave   **D** paid

12 This medicine should help, but if the problem .... come and see me again.
   A ocurs   **B** occurs   **C** recurs   **D** reccurs

13 It is .... likely that the government will back down and agree to the tax cuts.
   A completely   **B** fully   **C** highly   **D** totally

14 In 1990 the figures rose .... a previous high of 75% to a staggering 89%.
   A by   **B** from   **C** in   **D** with

15 The following year this figure .... noticeably from 72% to only 55%.
   A drop   **B** dropped   **C** dropping   **D** drops

16 There was a .... increase between 1989 and 2005.
   A significant   **B** significantly   **C** slightly   **D** steep

17 The bread .... baked in a hot oven and then put into bags ready for sale.
   A has   **B** is   **C** were   **D** can

18 We might be able to persuade more people to use the bus, but it is .... impossible to stop people from driving cars altogether.
   A absolutely   **B** highly   **C** very   **D** a little

19 There were losses in the car industry last year .... the tourism industry boomed.
   A in addition   **B** because   **C** similarly   **D** while

20 We made a significant profit last year .... the losses made by our international office.
   A although   **B** despite   **C** however   **D** as a result

21 I think school holidays are too long, ... I do think that children need more breaks than adults.
   A despite   **B** in spite of   **C** although   **D** furthermore

22 ...., I believe that banning smokers from public places is a very good idea.
   A Clearly   **B** Fortunately   **C** Justifiably   **D** Personally

23 A .... study has shown that fewer children are taking up smoking.
   A recnet   **B** recent   **C** rescent   **D** resent

24 The female birds eat very little food .... the males.
   A comparing to   **B** compared to   **C** comparing with   **D** comparing

25 Generally speaking, ... have totally different interests from older people.
   A kids   **B** guys   **C** youth   **D** the young

26 I am writing to .... for the position of tour guide advertised in your newsletter.
   A application   **B** apply   **C** invitation   **D** invite

27 I would be .... if you could send me a brochure.
   A greatful   **B** gratefull   **C** grateful   **D** greatfull

28 I really must apologise .... the way that I behaved during my stay at the hotel.
   A by   **B** for   **C** of   **D** to

29 I .... like to accept your kind offer of a free meal in your restaurant.
   A could   **B** can   **C** will   **D** would

30 I am really looking forward .... you again soon.
   A to seeing   **B** to see   **C** seeing   **D** see

Recording scripts

Recording 1a

Speaker A: On Mondays at school a group of us always talk about whatever movies we saw at the weekend. On Saturdays I often get together with my classmates and we see all the latest releases together. I can't remember the last time I saw a film with my parents – we just don't have much in common any more.

Speaker B: My parents are both teachers so you'd imagine I'd have no trouble at all academically. When I was little it was great because we had a really great relationship. But nowadays all we seem to do is argue and that causes a lot of conflict between us, so I don't really feel I can go to them for help. My friends aren't much help either as they've all got the same problem. Thank goodness I get on really well with my tutor at university. She's very approachable and, if I'm struggling with an assignment, I find her advice really helps me.

Speaker C: My parents are quite old so I feel as though they're out of touch with the modern world. They don't seem to have any idea of what things cost. I'm hoping to get a car in the next few months but I'll be taking my older brother along to help. We used to fight a lot when we were growing up but there's a really close bond between us now. He's already had a few cars so I'm sure he'll be a great help.

Speaker D: I play the violin and the piano and my grandad is a great cello player. A lot of my friends at school listen to all the popular bands and singers, but my tastes are totally different. I prefer classical music and they just don't understand it at all. Luckily Grandad shares my taste, so we often buy CDs and talk about them together.

Recording 1b

Teacher: Tell me about your family.

Student: Well, my immediate family is relatively small, just my parents, my two brothers and me. But both of my parents come from very large families so my extended family is very large – I have 25 cousins! Our family gatherings are pretty chaotic, but fun. We're a very close-knit family. Even though we don't live together any more, the family ties are still very strong. When we were little there wasn't very much sibling rivalry between us. I think it's because we had a very stable upbringing. Both of my parents played a very active role in our school life, and our home life, and they taught us to resolve our conflicts in a very fair way. I consider myself very lucky.

Teacher: Who are you most similar to in your family?

Student: Well, you can see a very clear family resemblance between my brothers and me, but everyone tells me that the physical resemblance between me and my maternal grandmother is very striking. Sadly, I never got to meet her because she died before I was born. But I've seen photographs of her at my age and we're quite alike. Other than that, I think I have my father's temperament – we're both very stubborn! But, thankfully, I also inherited his mathematical brain!

Teacher: And what do you think it takes to be a good parent?

Student: Well, I don't think just anyone can be a good parent. Not everyone has the right instincts. I think I have a very strong maternal instinct, because I love taking care of small children. So I hope to become a mother one day. I think it takes a great deal of patience and love.

Recording 1c

Narrator: You will hear the director of a child-care centre talking to the parent of a new child.

Director: Good morning, my name is Bob Ferguson and I'm the director of Ascot Child Care Centre.

Mother: Good morning, I'm Sallyanne Cullen. I made an appointment to enrol my daughter.

Director: That's right, I've got the application form right here. Now, first I need some personal details. So the family name is Cullen, is that right?

Mother: That's right.

Director: Now, what about your daughter, what does she like to be called?

Mother: Oh, her name is Alexandra, but we all just call her Alex, A-L-E-X.

Director: Great. As you know, we organise the children into different age groups. There's the babies' group, the toddlers, aged 2 to 3, and the pre-schoolers – they're aged 4 to 5. How old is your daughter?

Mother: Well, she'd go into the toddler group – she's just turned **three**.

Director: And we always like to make a note of our children's birthdays so we can celebrate it all together if they are at the centre on that day. When was she born?

Mother: Oh, erm, the 8 of November.

Director: Fine. And we also find it's a great help to know about siblings – sometimes, a problem at the centre can be related to problems with a sibling. Does she have any brothers or sisters?

Mother: Yes, a brother, Fraser. He's two years older.

Director: So that would make him five, is that right?

Mother: Yes, that's right.

Director: Fine. Now, we also need a contact address. Where do you live?

Mother: It's 108 Park Road, that's P-A-R-K, Maidstone.

Director: Good. Now, last of all, we need a telephone number we can call if there are any problems.

Mother: Oh, well, I'll be at work and so will my husband, so the best number to call is 34678890.

Director: Right, and is that a close relative?

Mother: Yes, it's my mother-in-law's number.

Director: We prefer to make a note of how the person is related to the child, so I'll write down 'grandmother'.

Mother: Yes, that does make more sense!

Director: Now, that's all of the personal details. We also like to try and get a picture of your child's personal development. Can you tell me if there are any specific problems she's having? For example, does she get on well with other children? Is sleeping a problem?

Mother: Oh, she gets on well with others, I think, but she does have trouble sleeping. We gave up her daytime nap a long time ago!

Director: That's good to know, I'll make a note of that. She can just have some quiet time while the others are resting if she likes.

Mother: That should be fine. She enjoys drawing quietly.

Director: Right. Now what about other skills? We occasionally take the children swimming, fully supervised of course, and we only go in a paddling pool as we don't expect them to swim by themselves yet. Does your daughter need a lot of help getting changed?

Mother: No, not at all. In fact she's been able to get dressed in the mornings for over a year now, so no problems there!

Director: That must be a big help for you! Now, what about the child-care arrangements? Are there any specific days you require?

Mother: Well, I work Monday to Wednesday, but my mother-in-law has agreed to look after her on Wednesdays.

Director: So does that mean that you'll just need Monday and Tuesday for now?

Mother: That's right.

Director: And what about the pick-up time? We offer extended hours for parents who work a great distance away.

Mother: Hmm … I work until 3 o'clock, but it takes me about half an hour to drive home, so ideally I'd like to pick her up at four if that's OK.

Director: That will be fine. Now is there any other information you'd like to…

Recording 2a

In the first years of a child's life many important milestones are reached. By the end of the first year a baby will have already *acquired* some social skills. He will enjoy *imitating* people and will also test parental responses to his behaviour. For example, what do my parents do if I refuse food? In terms of movement, an infant will be able to reach a sitting position *unassisted* and pull himself up to stand. He may be able to walk momentarily *without support*. As far as communication is concerned, he will be able to use simple gestures such as shaking his head for 'no', say 'mama' and 'dada' and he will try to imitate words. When it comes to cognitive development, he will be able to find hidden objects easily and use objects correctly such as drinking from a cup.

By the age of two or three, the infant has reached the toddler *stage*. In terms of social skills, this means, he is becoming more independent, which may result in the occasional tantrum. However, he has learned to take turns in games and *spontaneously* expresses affection. His physical development will also have increased significantly as he can now move around a lot faster and even run. He can also climb up stairs or onto relatively low obstacles, and even ride a small tricycle. However, he will still be rather unsteady on his feet at times. When it comes to language and communication he can now understand most sentences and uses four- and five-word sentences. In terms of cognitive development, he's learned to play make-believe games and uses his imagination more. He has also *mastered* the skill of sorting objects according to their shape and colour.

Between the ages of six and twelve, a child reaches what is termed 'middle childhood' and they will stay in this phase until they reach adolescence. In middle childhood, children's development is more affected by the outside world and the child's world expands to include friends, teachers, sports trainers and so on. Children develop at various rates and while some children in middle childhood seem very mature in terms of their emotional and social skills, others seem very immature. As far as physical milestones are concerned, during this stage growth is steady but less rapid than during the pre-school years. There are some major changes occurring at this stage as baby teeth will come out and permanent adult teeth will grow. As the mouth is not yet fully developed this may cause overcrowding. Eyes will reach maturity in both size and function. In terms of their cognitive ability, children at this stage master the skills of sequencing and ordering, which are essential for maths. By the end of this period children should have acquired effective reading and writing skills.

Recording 2b

Teacher: What do you remember about your early childhood?

Student: Oh, I remember being very happy! I have a lot of great memories of my childhood. In fact, my sisters and I often reminisce about it. Perhaps when you look back everything seems better, but our summer holidays seemed to go on forever and the sun always seemed to be shining. Nowadays, if we ever have a hot summer day, it always reminds me of my childhood holidays.

Teacher: Do you think you have a good memory or a poor memory?

Student: Well, when I was younger I think I used to have a very good memory. I used to be able to memorise long lists of dates without any trouble. But I find it harder and harder to remember things these days, so now I'd say my memory is quite poor. When I'm studying I find I have to think up strategies to help me, like visualising something associated with a particular word. I even forget important things sometimes, so I have to write myself little notes as a reminder.

Recording 3a

Narrator: Part 1

The heart is considered to be a muscle and, just like any other muscle in your body, your diet has a direct impact on the way that it works. The food you eat every day can affect the way that blood flows through your heart and arteries. A diet that is high in fat can gradually cause a build-up in your arteries that slows down the blood flow and can even block small arteries. If an artery that carries blood to the heart becomes blocked, the heart muscle can die. This is known as a heart attack and sufferers must receive treatment quickly. If the blockage occurs in an artery that carries blood to the brain, part of the brain can die. This is known as a stroke. The effects of a stroke can be debilitating and there is no known cure. The correct diet can help you control your weight and keep your arteries clear, thereby reducing the risk of heart problems and stroke.

Recording 3b

Narrator: Part 2

So, what can you do to lose weight? Well, exercise is by far the best way. Burning calories and working off the fat will help you look and feel better. Regular exercise helps you burn calories faster, even when you are sitting still. But what is the best type of exercise for your heart? Well, studies have shown that aerobic exercise causes you to breathe more deeply and makes your heart work harder to pump blood. Aerobic exercise also raises your heart rate and thus burns calories. Common examples of aerobic exercise include walking briskly, jogging, running, swimming and cycling.

People are often unsure just how much exercise they need. Again, recent studies can help. These have shown that it's best to begin slowly and gradually work up to 30 minutes of exercise, four to six times a week. However, your doctor may make a different recommendation based on your health. For example, it may be best to start with only a couple of minutes of exercise or begin at a fairly slow pace. If you are not used to exercise, be sure to pay careful attention to your body. One sure sign that you may be overdoing it is if you can't carry on a conversation while you exercise. To give your body the chance to recover, it's also best to alternate exercise days with rest days.

Recording 3c

bath, bathe, birth, breath, breathe, death, growth, health, mouth (v), mouth (n), teeth, teethe, writhe

Recording 3d

1   I took a deep breath before diving into the water.
2   The baby's crying because he's teething. He got two new teeth only yesterday.
3   Old people should take care of their health.
4   He's been so happy since the birth of his son.
5   The pain was so bad she was writhing in agony.
6   He can't breathe. You need to get him to hospital.

Recording 4a

Interviewer: Do you think people work too much nowadays?
Speaker 1: Not really, I think people have always worked hard for a living. I mean it's never been easy for anyone, has it? You have to work hard if you want to achieve anything in your life – that's just the way it is and there isn't a lot you can do about it. Life has its ups and downs and I think the best thing to do is accept that and get on with it.
Interviewer: What do you like to do to relax?
Speaker 2: For me there is only one way to relax and that's through sport. I like to live life on the edge, so I do a lot of extreme sports like paragliding and deep sea diving. When you're in a dangerous situation, that's when you really feel alive. I think your attitude has a big impact on your quality of life.
Interviewer: What's your idea of a perfect day?
Speaker 3: I don't think there's any such thing as the perfect day – something always seems to happen to spoil it. Some people say I have a negative attitude, but if I plan a picnic with friends then either it rains or my friends decide not to come along. I think it's a waste of time making plans like that. Life can be full of disappointments.
Interviewer: How would you describe your attitude to life?
Speaker 4: I have a very positive outlook on life. I think it's important to treat every day as special and live life to the full. Some people approach everything as if their glass is half empty. If you do that then it will colour every experience you have. I think if you want to lead a happy life then you need to have a positive approach to everything.

Recording 4b

Narrator: You will hear a woman talking on the radio about things for children to do during the school holidays.

The school holidays are fast approaching and I'm sure all of you parents out there are worried about how to occupy your children. Well, I have a few tips that may help keep your children entertained without spending large amounts of money. One of our biggest problems is that today's children often do not have the type of hobby that was familiar in the past, such as making their own toys. Instead they rely on sophisticated video games to keep them amused. But children also like to feel needed, so why not give them jobs to do around the house? You may be surprised how much they will enjoy simple tasks such as washing your car. Another idea is to use this time to develop their cooking skills. Food is something we all enjoy, so why not get them to prepare some simple dishes in the kitchen? Learning to cook is a useful life skill for children to learn and it can also keep them happy for several hours.

Children also love doing arts and crafts, so why not give them the task of making presents for upcoming birthdays or celebrations? Not only will they enjoy making them but you'll also save some money and the family or friends who receive the gifts are sure to be delighted. A great idea to get children out of the house is to find out about how they can help in your local community. Perhaps there is a home for the elderly nearby. They are sure to welcome a visit from young people – even a few minutes a week can brighten their day. Of course younger children cannot do these things for very long, but older ones may find that there are ongoing projects around your neighbourhood that they can help with.

These are just a few ideas, but I'm sure you can think of many more. If not, there are plenty of places to look for other suggestions. Nowadays the first place people seem to look is the Internet, which can be a good source of information. However, it does have its limits because ideas suitable for children living in the city may not translate well for children in rural areas. So don't overlook your library. These are often filled with great ideas targeted at children in your specific area. There are a few key points to remember, however. One of the most important things is to keep your children active, otherwise they will be sure to get bored. Also remember that, although children can be very independent even from nine or ten years old, you should still be there to take care of them up to the age of twelve. So don't be tempted to let older children babysit their younger siblings. This should only be done by an adult.

Recording 5a

Teacher: Can you tell me about your early education?
Student: Well, I went to kindergarten from the age of four and I remember that I didn't enjoy it very much at all. Primary school was a little better, especially because my mum was a teacher in the school. She taught in the junior part of the school and she was actually my teacher in first grade but when I went up to the senior school I didn't see very much of her. After that I was lucky enough to receive a scholarship to go to a very good high school. My parents couldn't have afforded to send me to a private school so it was a really great opportunity for me. It was a single-sex school so there were no boys. I'm glad I didn't go to a mixed school because I think there are fewer distractions so everyone can just concentrate on their studies.

Recording 5b

So you have graduated from university and decided to continue studying towards a Master's or PhD. At some stage during the next few years will need to consider your thesis. One of the greatest difficulties faced by postgraduate students is choosing a topic to base their dissertation on. Writing a thesis can be very daunting, but the task is much more straightforward if the topic you select is appropriate for you. So, what can you do to solve this problem?

Well there are several things to keep in mind. Firstly you need to do your research so that you are very familiar with all the current literature. On top of this, you also need to be sure that you have a broad knowledge of your area of specialisation. If you do this, it will help you with the next important point in choosing a good subject for your research, which is to ascertain what is relevant in your research area. This will be crucial in helping you to narrow your choices down. From the very beginning, it really is vital to set clear limits and to have a very fixed plan in terms of the scope of your research.

It can be even more helpful to analyse existing research and ask yourself if there are any controversies. Perhaps there is a theory that you may want to challenge and this could be the focus of your study. A further and very important factor to take into account is your own financial resources. If these are limited then you need to avoid choosing a study that will involve costly equipment or surveys. However, if this is the case, you needn't despair or abandon your ideas altogether, instead make enquiries into funding from external agencies such as your local government. You may even find that local industries are willing to support your research by providing a grant. It's always worth looking around to see just what is possible. And finally, be sure to make good use of your tutor, especially when it comes to making sure that your findings are accurate.

Recording 5c

academic, assignment, consideration, concentrate, controversy, controversy (both are possible), conduct, distraction, dissertation, economist, educational, educated, research (n), thesis, theory, theoretical

Recording 6a

I'm a French teacher, but I remember when I first started to learn the language I really struggled with it. I didn't really have a problem with the pronunciation like the other kids in my class, I was just overwhelmed by all of the vocabulary. But I persevered and soon I was scoring ten out of ten in all of the tests. By the time I got to university I could produce essays and translate eighteenth century texts without much difficulty and I actually enjoyed learning the grammar rules. Then, as part of my university course I had to go and live in France for a year. That's when I learned that communication was more important than accuracy. As soon as I arrived I realised I didn't know how to order the type of coffee I liked, and trying to find accommodation was a nightmare. I called people about ads in the paper, but I had to keep putting the phone down because I couldn't understand a word they were saying - they all spoke so quickly! There was a very real language barrier. I could see then that there's no point in just knowing words if you can't hold a conversation with a native speaker. Fluency is what helps you to function properly – it's what helps you get a job, hold a conversation or just buy the things you need.

Recording 6b

Teacher: What do you think you need to do to be a good language learner?

Student: Well, you need to be able to put down your textbooks from time to time and forget about accuracy. That's the only way to become more fluent in a language. You also need to speak to native speakers of the language as much as you can.

Teacher: What do you think makes a good language teacher?

Student: I think the best language teachers are those who can speak another language themselves. Teachers also need to be able to explain things clearly and in a way that is easy to follow.

Teacher: What problems do people experience when learning your language?

Student: My first language is very difficult to learn because of the pronunciation. The individual sounds are very strange to other nationalities and often difficult for them to pronounce.

Recording 7a

Speaker 1: I live in a quaint little village about 300 kilometres from the nearest big city. Although it's a long way, the drive from the city is well worth the effort because the surrounding countryside is very scenic. I like living here because it's so peaceful and the air is really fresh, so it's much nicer than in the city. It's a pretty sleepy village, but on Sundays there's a huge market and people come from all the neighbouring villages to buy and sell their local produce.

Speaker 2: The most popular part of my hometown is the beach. We have long stretches of white sand and the water is crystal clear. The sea can be very calm at times but the surf can also be spectacular. Visitors who enjoy water sports are really well catered for as you can go snorkelling, scuba diving and deep-sea fishing. Soon we're going to get our own airport but for now people can only get here by ferry.

Speaker 3: My city is famous for its skyscrapers, statues and fountains - but most of all for its shopping! You can buy anything you want here and we have over fifty large shopping malls. We get a lot of overseas visitors, so our airport is one of the busiest in the world. It's a very exciting and cosmopolitan place to live. Most people don't drive because there are always traffic jams, but the public transport is really well organised. We have some great attractions nearby for visitors, as well as a huge sports stadium and fantastic theme parks. I suppose the only downside is that the air can get a little polluted at times.

Speaker 4: My village is 200 metres above sea level and we overlook the villages and lakes down in the valley below. It's very picturesque up here so we get a lot of visitors, especially artists who want to paint the landscape. They also like our traditional houses. The air is very crisp up here as well, so a lot of people come up here to escape the heat in the city. The roads are pretty treacherous because they're very steep and winding, so most people arrive by train. The scenery on the way up here really is breathtaking.

Recording 7b

boundary, bought, cough, country, course, double, doubt, drought, enough, journal, journey, nought, rough, south, southern, tourism, tourist, trouble, trough

Recording 8a

Speaker 1: I must say I'm never on time. In fact, I was late for meetings three days in a row last week. Everyone's always angry with me because I do tend to keep people waiting a lot. Work is my problem – I get so engrossed that I lose all track of time. I try to get everything else ready before I start, which saves a bit of time, but before I know it a few hours have passed and I'm already late.

Speaker 2: I can't say I'm very punctual. I do my best not to be late because I hate being kept waiting myself, but I do sometimes spend too much time getting ready. If I'm going out somewhere I like to plait my hair, which is very thick so this can be very time-consuming and I often have to rush through everything else I need to do. I once went to a wedding and I took so long doing my hair that I only just arrived in time to hear the bride say 'I do'.

Speaker 3: I could tell the time at a very early age and I've been obsessed with punctuality ever since! I own about 12 watches and clocks, but none of them show the right time. I can't stand to be late for work or in a hurry, so I make sure they're all ten minutes fast - and I always carry a spare watch in case one of them stops! That way I always arrive at meetings in plenty of time and I can take my time getting my paperwork ready.

Recording 8b

Welcome once again to 'Introduction to dentistry' and in today's lecture we'll be looking at the history of dentistry through the ages. Now, skulls of the Cro-Magnon people who inhabited the Earth 25,000 years ago show evidence of tooth decay and the earliest recorded mention of oral disease was in 5000 BC. This proves that oral disease is by no means a modern-day problem and has in fact plagued humans since time began. That particular reference appeared in a text written by the ancient people of Sumeria, which referred to 'tooth worms'. There is also evidence that dental problems caused difficulties in other early civilizations and people from those times actually developed treatments for them. For example, we have found historical evidence that the Chinese used acupuncture to treat the pain associated with tooth decay. There is even further evidence of the troubles caused by toothache in the Ebers Papyrus, which is a text written between 1700 and 1500 BC by the people of ancient Egypt. This papyrus contains references to diseases of the teeth, as well as prescriptions for medications they used at that time. While today we automatically prescribe antibiotics, the ancient Egyptians relied on more traditional remedies to help with tooth decay. Firstly, olive oil, which even today is known to have therapeutic qualities and secondly, onions, which again are an age-old traditional medicine and are still recognized as a reliable source of natural antibiotics.

A large proportion of early dentistry was practised as a part of general medicine. However, by the fifth century BC, Herodotus, a Greek historian, made the following observation: 'In Egypt, medicine is practiced on a plan of separation – each physician treats a single disorder and no more. Some undertake to cure diseases of the eye, others the head and others again, of the teeth.' The Greeks were at the forefront of dentistry of that time and it was a Greek physician who lived between 1300 and 1200 BC who chose to extract problem teeth long before anyone else. Arabs were also pioneers in the area of oral hygiene and used a small polishing stick as a toothbrush as early as 100BC.

So, what of Europe? Well, throughout the Middle Ages, dentistry was made available to the wealthier classes thanks to physicians who would visit individuals in their home, while dentistry for the poorer people took place in the market place. Italian sources from the 1400s mention the use of gold leaf as dental filling material, but it was a Frenchman, Pierre Fauchard, who is credited with being the father of modern dentistry, thanks to his book *The Surgeon Dentist: a treatise on teeth*, which describes basic oral anatomy and the signs and symptoms of tooth decay.

Recording 9a

The meerkat is found exclusively on the semi-arid plains of southern Africa. In terms of its natural environment, the meerkat avoids woodland and dense vegetation. At night, the meerkat retires to a network of burrows, which it digs with its powerful forelegs. If rocky ground makes this impossible, the meerkat will make its den in the crevices between the rocks.

Meerkats feed mainly on insects, spiders and snails, but their diet occasionally includes small rodents, lizards and the roots of certain plants. They will even tackle dangerous prey such as scorpions and snakes. Relying on its keen sense of smell, the meerkat is a successful forager.

Recording 9b

adapt, agriculture, catastrophe, chemical, climate, disastrous, endangered, genetically, human, natural, vulnerable

Recording 10a

Many people believe that one day we will form a colony on another planet. Today we're going to look at some other planets and consider why it will never be feasible for humans to live on them.

Let's start with Venus. Now, Venus is unusual because it rotates in a different direction to the other planets orbiting the sun. In terms of its physical features it's similar in size to Earth. However, unlike Earth, it doesn't have any oceans. It's also extremely hot, thanks to the thick covering of cloud, which keeps the heat at 484 degrees centigrade. This cloud also reflects sunlight, which is why Venus appears so bright from Earth. A further problem is the continual thunderstorms, which could make life there rather unpleasant. The surface of Venus also has many craters as a result of asteroid collisions.

Next is Mercury, which is a third of the size of our planet. In fact, it's smaller than all the other planets, except Pluto. Life would be difficult there because it's close to the sun and has almost no atmosphere. On Mercury the temperature varies more than on any other planet in the solar system and, as it has no water, it is unable to sustain life.

Let's consider Saturn next. We know a lot more about Saturn nowadays, thanks to the Voyager space shuttle, which taught us a lot about the rings around Saturn. We also know that Saturn has a large number of moons. Saturn has barely any solid surface, as its composition is mostly gas. It is also extremely hot, making life for humans impossible.

Recording 10b

astronaut, atmosphere, commercial, explorer, exploration, galaxy, horizon, horizontal, outer, satellite, solar system, sustain, universal

Recording 10c

Narrator: You will hear two science lecturers discussing space exploration.

Susan: Hello, John. How was your conference on space travel?

John: Hi, Susan. It was great. We heard some fascinating speakers, especially one fellow who was an expert on Mars. He thinks it's quite feasible for humans to live there in the near future.

Susan: Well, if we spent the billions of dollars that go into space research on looking after our own planet, then perhaps we wouldn't need to worry about the Earth being uninhabitable in a hundred years' time. Nor would we need to look for another planet to colonise!

John: Yes, but there are some important things that space exploration can teach us, you know, especially about the history of our own planet and its atmosphere. That sort of knowledge could help us solve some of the problems that threaten our planet.

Susan: Still, I don't really see why they have to send astronauts into space. Robotics is so much more advanced now, why can't they simply send robots?

John: Well, robotics has come a long way and it is more expensive to send a manned spaceship into orbit, but the biggest problem with robots is that they have to be programmed for every possible eventuality.

Susan: Yes, I suppose you're right. Robots just can't react to situations independently the way that humans do - they still need us to tell them what to do.

John: That's right. Robots may have come a long way, but if you're going to go to all the expense of building one, you really need to make sure it's going to work when it gets there and they don't tend to take risks with new and untested technology. What if it lets you down? So, instead, a lot of the space technology nowadays is actually based on the technology they used in the 1970s, because we know that it works and it's reliable.

Susan: So do you think it will ever be possible to send robots to Mars?

John: I'm not sure. One of the speakers spoke about that, and he says that communication would be a problem.

Susan: Is that because of the conditions? I mean those extremes of temperature and even the atmosphere itself, would probably create an awful lot of interference.

John: Yes, but they're both issues that can be dealt with. No, the real problem is simply how far away it is. That would cause long delays before the robots received any messages about what to do next, so for the moment they don't think it's feasible.

Susan: Hmm, that makes sense. But, tell me, do you really think we should be contemplating sending humans to Mars at all? Don't you think we should wait until we do have the technology?

John: Well, many years ago the civilisations that built the pyramids or that began building enormous cathedrals must have started the project never expecting to see it finished. I think we should take the same approach and start our preparations now.

Susan: That's an interesting point, though I'm still not convinced. Surely you don't foresee a time when humans will be living on Mars, that's just science fiction, isn't it?

John: Not at all. I think there is a distinct possibility that humans will live there.

Susan: But what about the conditions there? Even the dirt on the ground could kill us.

John: Yes, I agree with you there, but we can easily build a self-contained structure there so people don't need to go outside.

Susan: Mm, I suppose the ground does also contain a lot of resources, so getting metals wouldn't be a problem.

John: That's right. A lot of building materials could be found there. But there are still many risks involved.

Susan: Yes, what about radiation? I don't think there will ever be a way to shield us totally from cosmic radiation. Even inside a spaceship.

John: I can't agree with you there. Astronauts have been travelling in space for a long time now, so that shouldn't be too much of a problem for us.

Susan: I just don't think we have enough experience of living in space long-term.

John: But you have to accept that it is within the realms of possibility that one day there will be a Martian space station.

Susan: Well, I have every faith in science and Mars does seem to be the next frontier. So, yes, I imagine we will eventually send a space mission there, but I can't see people living there.

Recording 11a

Speaker A: I live in a cottage. It's a single-storey building so the rooms are all on the same level. It's about a hundred years old and it's a very traditional design, so there's no concrete or steel to be found. Just about all the buildings in this area were built from timber and stone from the local quarry. It's got a lot of character. What I like best about it are the ceilings. They're quite ornate as they have lots of pretty details on them. Although some people think it's small, I prefer to think of it as cosy.

Speaker B: My flat is in a new high-rise building in the city centre. The design is ultra-modern, so there's a lot of glass and concrete and steel - and not a lot of wood to be seen. Everything is controlled through a state-of-the-art computer system. It's a very functional apartment and there's a space to suit every purpose, but I do find the bedrooms a bit cramped. My favourite spot is the balcony - my building towers over everything else, so I can see for miles.

Speaker C: I live in a two-storey house. It's a very conventional brick building and it's typical of the area where I live. I love the downstairs rooms as they're very spacious. I spend a lot of time in the living room because it's so light and airy. But my favourite feature is definitely the staircase. It curves around at the bottom and just seems to invite you to climb it.

Recording 11b

design, please, device, devise, residence, housing, fasten, destruction, use (n), use (v)

Recording 12a

Woman: I can't decide between the Smart Phone and the Optima. Which one do you think is better?

Assistant: Well, I prefer the Smart Phone because it's so compact. I find the Optima a bit bulky. Although I have to say that the size of the Smart Phone does make it tricky to operate, whereas the Optima is very user-friendly.

Woman: Why do you think that is?

Assistant: Well, the Smart Phone has a standard telephone keypad and I find them really awkward to use when I'm sending messages. The Optima opens up to reveal a full keyboard inside. You can also scroll up and down by touching the screen. I like the way the

Smart Phone automatically displays a calendar when you open it up though, that's a really useful function.

Woman: Can they both connect to the Internet?

Assistant: Yes, they're both equipped with the latest technology. But I find the Optima downloads information a lot faster and it also has a bigger memory, so it can store more data.

Recording 12b

Speaker A: I wash my hair every morning so the gadget I use most is my ... you know, the thing you use to dry your hair.

Speaker B: I mainly use my computer as a ... you know, to do processing of the things I need to write.

Speaker C: One gadget I really want to buy is a machine to blend up food so I can make my own healthy drinks.

Speaker D: I'm not very good at adding up big numbers so I can't imagine what it was like before they had ... you know, those machines that can do it for you.

Speaker E: My mother still washes the dishes by hand and it takes her a long time. I'd like to get a machine that can do the job for her.

Recording 13a

Bill: Just look at this, they're putting one of those cheap restaurant chains in where that nice tea-shop used to be. They're owned by some multinational company. At this rate our culture will disappear altogether and we'll all end up eating the same bland food.

Amy: Well, a lot of people are worried about globalisation and the impact it could have on the local people. But actually I'm beginning to think it works the other way around.

Bill: You can't be serious.

Amy: Yes, I'm reading a book about it actually and the author makes some very valid points.

Bill: He probably works for one of the big multinationals himself!

Amy: Actually, no. I'm pretty sure he's a journalist.

Bill: So, what does he say then?

Amy: Well, he points out that there are far more ethnic restaurants in England than people realise, for example, there are seven Indian restaurants for every one McDonald's in the UK.

Bill: Really? I didn't realise that.

Amy: Yes, and globally, pizzas are actually more popular than burgers. I think globalisation could mean that we end up living a more interesting and multicultural life.

Bill: Yes, but you've got to admit that, worldwide, the soft drinks market is totally dominated by just one or two big companies.

Amy: Well, according to this author, there's a new energy drink taking over the market and it's a joint venture between Thailand and Austria. Without globalisation, international companies just wouldn't merge like that.

Bill: Well I think that globalisation just pushes popular culture to the masses and spreads it even further. When people go travelling to far flung places, they want to see something exotic, not the same icons they see all around them at home!

Amy: Yes, but I doubt the local people there feel they're losing their national identity just because a fast food outlet has opened up. And anyway, the nice thing about it is that, in many places, these chains have to change the food they sell to suit the local culture. So there is a lot of give and take going on and you still get cultural diversity to some extent.

Bill: I suppose so. I suppose so. I guess no one big multinational has a monopoly over the fashion market either, does it?

Amy: That's right, the big fashion labels are spread over a lot of different countries.

Recording 13b

global, globalisation, implication, isolation, culture, domestic, international, local, sceptical, modernisation, national, multicultural, projection

Recording 14a

Mary: Hi, Jean. You look worried. Is everything OK?

Jean: Hi, Mary. Actually I'm facing a few problems at work and I'm not really sure how to deal with them.

Mary: What sort of problems?

Jean: Well, we've just got a new boss and he's expecting us to start work at 8 o'clock in the morning. Of course that's causing problems for me at home because it means my husband has to take the children to school every morning, which is making him late for work.

Mary: Oh dear. I know how you feel. I had to deal with a similar problem last year.

Jean: How did you tackle it?

Mary: Well, I didn't at first and that created an even worse situation. The traffic is so bad nowadays that I was leaving the house at 6:30 every morning to get there in time. Eventually I realised I would have to address the problem sooner or later, so I raised the issue with my boss.

Jean: Did you manage to resolve it?

Mary: Yes, he was terrific. He said he hadn't realised that the early start would present a problem and he agreed to let me start half an hour later.

Jean: That's great, I'm sure my boss has no idea how much trouble he's caused. Perhaps I should deal with it the same way.

Mary: Well, they say that identifying the problem is the hardest part. Tackling it should be the easy part.

Jean: You haven't met my new boss!

Recording 14b

accepted, crowded, developed, excluded, included, isolated, overpriced, overworked, resolved, stressed, solved

Recording 15a

Narrator: Statement 1

Speaker A: I think it could be beneficial to educate the public this way. Anything we do to raise awareness of these issues is very worthwhile. The more educated people are, the more advantageous it is for the environment.

Speaker B: I honestly think it would be pointless. People just don't read leaflets, so handing them out would be futile. Not only would it be a fruitless exercise, but it would also create more litter!

Narrator: Statement 2

Speaker A: I think this is an unattainable goal. I think it would prove impracticable even to think about trying to achieve this. Our environmental problems are so great now that it's unfeasible to imagine that we could solve all our pollution problems so quickly.

Speaker B: Look, I think everyone in my country is so aware of the impact we're having on the environment that I think it is conceivable that we'll have solved the problem soon. It's quite feasible that we'll all be driving electric cars. They're a viable alternative to petrol-driven cars, so getting rid of pollution is definitely achievable.

Narrator: Statement 3

Speaker A: I think it's improbable that everyone will abandon the chemicals we're using now. So many people have been using them for years and it's questionable whether they will be able to convince everyone to stop. Yeah, I'd say this one is very doubtful.

Speaker B: There are a lot of great cleaning products now that are eco-friendly and I think governments are liable to start putting pressure on manufacturers to produce more products like these. I think it's quite probable that within ten years everyone will have made the switch.

Recording 15b

1 I refuse to go.
2 Disposing of refuse is a growing problem.
3 There is a conflict here.
4 The two reports conflict each other.
5 We all need to be present at the meeting.
6 This issue presents an enormous problem.
7 We are making a lot of progress.
8 We need to progress at a faster rate.
9 There has been an increase in carbon emissions.
10 Temperatures are expected to increase.

Recording 16

Let's find out just how environmentally aware you are.

Question one. How many trees do you think it would take to offset the CO_2 emissions from a long distance flight? Well, it's estimated that for each mile or 1.6 km that a jet flies, half a kilo of CO_2 is added to the atmosphere. So a round trip of 10,000 miles would emit about one and a half tonnes of CO_2 per passenger. The amount of CO_2 a tree can absorb depends on factors such as its type, location and age. The company, Future Forests, says that, on average, it would take two trees 99 years to counter the effect of this trip, so the answer here is C.

Question two. What is the most environmentally friendly way to wash your clothes? Well, the solvents used by most dry cleaners are damaging to the environment. In a washing machine, the vast majority of the energy – about 90 per cent of it - goes into heating up the water, not running through the cycle. Washing clothes in hot water, even by hand, uses a lot of energy to heat the water. Keeping washing temperatures low and always washing a full load is the best policy. So the correct answer is C.

Question three. Do you need to always turn off your electric lights to save energy? It is a common myth that flicking the lights on and off uses more energy than leaving them on. In fact an ordinary bulb only has to be turned off for three seconds to outweigh the cost of turning it back on. For energy efficient and other fluorescent bulbs, this rises to five minutes. Energy efficient light bulbs use 75 per cent less energy than ordinary ones – so if you have those, but leave them on as you tidy - you'll probably still use less energy than if you switch your standard bulbs on and off. So the correct answer is B.

Question four. What is the most energy efficient way of cooking a baked potato? A microwave uses just a third of the electricity required to operate an electric oven, and of course the potato will take much less time to cook, so the correct answer is B.

Question five. What is the best way to help reduce your CO_2 emissions throughout the year? Well, it's estimated that one person taking the train for a year, rather than driving a car, would reduce their CO_2 emission total by 2.9 tonnes. Hanging out your washing rather than using a tumble dryer would cut CO_2 by 0.9 tonnes and working from home one day a week would cut 0.88 tonnes. So the correct answer is A.

Recording 17a

Speaker 1: I'm a student so I only work part-time. I managed to get a job as a shelf stocker in the local supermarket. It's unskilled work and very monotonous, but the pay is quite good. Every week when I get my wages I put them straight into the bank. I'm saving up for a new computer. I've nearly got enough, which is just as well because my prospects aren't good - I think they're going to make me redundant next month!

Speaker 2: My occupation is receptionist at a five-star hotel. I got the job while I was studying. We had to complete part of our course in the workplace, and this is where I was placed. It's a very demanding job and I have to do shift work, which I find exhausting. The perks are great though. I get to stay in luxurious hotels around the world for next to nothing and I get on really well with all the other staff. My father worked in this industry all his life. He retired the same year that I started.

Speaker 3: I work as a labourer on a construction site. It's manual work, so it's very physical, which keeps me nice and fit. My wages aren't great, but I often get to do a lot of overtime, so I can earn more money that way.

Speaker 4: I've always wanted a career in marketing, so I studied as a graphic designer and when I graduated I got a job with a marketing company. I had to compete against some very good candidates to get the job, so I was really pleased. I've recently been promoted and now I'm in charge of several advertising campaigns. I find the job really rewarding, and that's not just because of the great salary. I get to use the skills I learned at college. I also get on very well with my colleagues. Job satisfaction is really important to me.

Recording 17b

bird, earn, first, nurse, perk, purse, work
park, clerk, market, target
ball, floor, law, poor, walk, force

Recording 18

In spite of the large number of prisons we have, crime figures have risen again this year with the number of drug-related crimes in particular increasing. Many law-abiding citizens believe that our existing laws are just not tough enough and do not act as enough of a deterrent against crime. In recent years there has been a move to abolish laws which were deemed to be too harsh or strict and to reduce the punishment for non-violent crimes, such as those against property. On the other hand, in some countries the police can enforce laws against crossing the street at the wrong place by imposing a fine.

Laws like this are passed simply to keep us safe and some see them as an intrusion on our privacy. Focusing on petty crimes in this way can also cause people who generally obey the law to resent the police rather than respect them for what they do. They would rather their time was spent solving more serious crimes. It's difficult to believe that reducing punishments will help to combat crime. It goes without saying that laws against serious crimes should be strictly enforced. However, we also need to focus more attention on crime prevention and educating young people to abide by the law. They need to know that no one is above the law and there are serious consequences if they're involved in criminal activities in any way. Some people believe that non-violent crimes or so-called victimless crimes such as fraud should be punished less. However, there is always a victim somewhere, even if that victim is a company and its owners. And victims often feel the effects of a crime for many years, whether the attack is planned or random. Perhaps it's time to start introducing new laws rather than abolishing them.

Recording 19a

Good morning, my name is Dan Taylor and I'm Professor of Sociology here at Manly University.

Our modern society often prides itself on its free press and, with access to the Internet and cable television the news is broadcast 24 hours a day. However, we have just completed a study which reveals that the general public is increasingly ill-informed today. For this project we compiled a list of what we considered to be the most significant current affairs stories and then we assessed how these stories were reported by newspapers and radio and television networks. Alarmingly, we found that as many as 25 significant news stories were either under-reported or omitted from the news altogether.

It would seem that the media today seeks to entertain rather than inform the public. I define censorship as anything which interferes with the free flow of information in our society. And this would seem to be what tabloid journalism is doing. They are effectively censoring important news stories on the basis that they may not be interesting or entertaining enough. One example is the widening gap between the rich and the poor. This is a major problem in big cities today and yet you are unlikely to find a reference to it in any news headlines. Instead, you're more likely to find stories about the latest celebrity, with important news content relegated to the back pages.

Recording 19b

Teacher: Would you like to be famous?

Student: I think a lot of people want to be famous nowdays and that's why reality TV is so popular. But I wouldn't like to be famous at all. Being famous nowadays simply means that you're in the tabloids a lot and you're followed by the paparazzi everywhere you go. I'd find that very intrusive. Famous people have no privacy at all in any part of their life. Their life also seems to be very superficial because they spend all of their time going to parties and trying to look glamorous. It all seems very artificial to me – they just don't seem to be part of the real world at all.

Teacher: Hmm. Do you think famous people have a positive or a negative influence on young people?

Student: I think they should have a positive influence on young people, but many of them don't. Some personalities are good role

models and use their celebrity status to encourage people to think about important issues, but we often see photos of famous people behaving badly.

Teacher: Nowadays we have access to the news 24 hours a day. What effect does this have?

Student: I think it can affect us in both positive and negative ways. On the one hand, it's very convenient to be able to catch up with what's happening in the world at any time of the day or night, no matter where you are. But on the other hand, this kind of news can give you a distorted view of what's happening, because even minor news stories are given more importance than they perhaps should have.

Recording 19c

artificial, attention, biased, censor, exposed, exposure, intrusive, intrusion, invasion, invasive, publication, superficial

Recording 20a

For those of you who are interested in aesthetics, why not consider a visit to Bethania Island this year? The island will host three arts festivals, each one showcasing different areas of the art world. First, there is Living Writers' Week. Throughout the week there will be talks by local and international writers and a chance to dine with them at the various literary lunches. You'll also be able to pick up old and new editions at the very large book fair. The little ones haven't been forgotten and so there are plenty of children's activities planned as well. As is the case each year, there will be a theme for the festival and this year it is *Island life*.

Later in the year, there will be a celebration of the visual arts. There are some very famous and accomplished painters in residence on the island and their work will be featured in a wonderful exhibition. Works by Alex Green, whose paintings depict the beautiful scenery this island is famous for, will be a prominent feature. Visitors to the festival will get the chance to discuss the creative process with the artists and there will also be opportunities to try out your own artistic skills at the workshops being held at various galleries on the island. To top it all off, there will be a display of crafts created by emerging artists. You'll be amazed at the intricate wooden carvings produced by local craftsmen.

And finally, if you love music then you shouldn't miss the Festival of Voices. You will be able to hear performers from around the world. What makes this even more interesting is that some of this year's performances are going to be interactive so members of the audience will be invited to participate as well. One of the stages will be devoted to showcasing musical theatre and the good news is that there will be plenty of free concerts for everyone to enjoy.

Recording 20b

My taste in music is quite eclectic and there isn't really one style of music that I like. I listen to everything from popular music to classical. Music plays a very important role in my life, and I listen to it almost constantly. I find that it helps to set or to change a mood. So I tend to choose my music according to who I'm with or what I'm doing. For example, if I'm driving long distances in my car I prefer to play something stimulating to help keep me awake. But if I'm having a dinner party with friends, then I play something more relaxing. I think that music helps to inspire me when I'm working, although my colleagues find it distracting so I tend to listen with headphones on. In that way I can escape into my own little world. When I was younger I would definitely have said that I preferred live music. The atmosphere in a live concert can be electric. Nowadays, though, a lot of popular groups only perform at very large venues in front of audiences of 20,000 or more and I don't really like that. I prefer the intimacy of listening to recorded music and the sound quality is better as well. Music really enriches our lives - it can turn a boring, monotonous period of time into a magical experience, so I think it's essential to have music and, in fact, all of the arts in your life.

Recording 20c

atmosphere, classical, edition, festival, fundamental, imagination, literary, monotonous, musical, performance, popular, visual

Recording 21

put, these, in, some, ball, choose, word, about, guest, what, attack, hard

Recording 22a

1   analysis, analyse, analytical
2   benefit, benefit, beneficial
3   consistency, consist, consistent
4   creation, creator, creativity, create, creative
5   definition, define, definable, definitive, definite
6   environment, environmentalist, environmental
7   occurrence, occur
8   period, periodical, periodic
9   significance, signify, significant
10 theory, theorise, theoretical

Recording 22b

A   Leading environmentalists are concerned about the effects our modern lifestyle is having on global warming.
B   Scientists have shown that including fish in our diet may be beneficial in reducing heart disease.
C   Satellites have recently sent back important new data from Mars, although it is not yet clear what significance the findings have for future space exploration.
D   Young children are often very creative, although many give up art when they begin high school.
E   Your essay is good, but you need to define the causes of pollution more clearly.
F   I prefer teachers who don't put too much emphasis on learning and studying the theory of chemistry. I'm much more interested in the practical side of things.
G   The student council consists of ten undergraduates and four postgraduate students.
H   After you've planted your seeds you can't simply leave them to grow, they do need to be checked periodically for weeds and pests.
I   We analysed the test results to see whether there really is a link between video games and increased violence.
J   The torrential storm last night seems to be part of a pattern – a similar storm occurred two years ago following a severe drought.

Wordlist

UNIT 1

GROWING UP

Nouns

adolescence /ˌædəl'esənts/
adulthood /'ædʌlthʊd/
bond /bɒnd/
brotherhood /'brʌðəhʊd/
character /'kærəktə/
childhood /'tʃaɪldhʊd/
conflict /'kɒnflɪkt/
connection /kə'nekʃən/
fatherhood /'fɑːðəhʊd/
friendship /'frendʃɪp/
instinct /'ɪnstɪŋkt/
interaction /ˌɪntə'rækʃən/
motherhood /'mʌðəhʊd/
nature /'neɪtʃə/
parent /'peərənt/
relation /rɪ'leɪʃən/
relationship (between/with)
    /rɪ'leɪʃənʃɪp/
relative /'relətɪv/
resemblance /rɪ'zembləns/
rivalry /'raɪvəlri/
sibling /'sɪblɪŋ/
teenager /'tiːnˌeɪdʒə/
temperament /'tempərəmənt/
ties /taɪz/
upbringing /'ʌpbrɪŋɪŋ/

Compound nouns

active role
extended family
family gathering
immediate family
maternal instinct
sibling rivalry
stable upbringing
striking resemblance

Adjectives

close /kləʊs/
close-knit /ˌkləʊs'nɪt/
maternal /mə'tɜːnəl/
parental /pə'rentəl/
rewarding /rɪ'wɔːdɪŋ/
stable /'steɪbl/

Verbs

accommodate /ə'kɒmədeɪt/
adopt /ə'dɒpt/
break down /breɪk daʊn/
develop /dɪ'veləp/
endure /ɪn'djʊə/
establish /ɪ'stæblɪʃ/

have sth in common
inherit /ɪn'herɪt/
interact /ˌɪntə'rækt/
nurture /'nɜːtʃə/
play a role
relate (to) /rɪ'leɪt/

UNIT 2

MENTAL AND PHYSICAL DEVELOPMENT

Nouns

ability /ə'bɪləti/
adolescent /ˌædəl'esənt/
behaviour /bɪ'heɪvjə/
childhood /'tʃaɪldhʊd/
concept /'kɒnsept/
consequence /'kɒnsɪkwəns/
gesture /'dʒestʃə/
growth /grəʊθ/
height /haɪt/
imagination /ɪˌmædʒɪ'neɪʃən/
infancy /'ɪnfənsi/
infant /'ɪnfənt/
knowledge /'nɒlɪdʒ/
maturity /mə'tjʊərəti/
memory /'meməri/
milestone /'maɪlstəʊn/
mind /maɪnd/
peers /pɪəz/
period /'pɪəriəd/
phase /feɪz/
rate /reɪt/
reminder /rɪ'maɪndə/
social skills
skill /skɪl/
stage /steɪdʒ/
toddler /'tɒdlə/
transition /træn'zɪʃən/

Adjectives

abstract /'æbstrækt/
cognitive /'kɒgnətɪv/
clumsy /'klʌmzi/
fond /fɒnd/
fully-grown /'fʊli grəʊn/
immature /ˌɪmə'tjʊə/
independent /ˌɪndɪ'pendənt/
irresponsible /ˌɪrɪ'spɒnsəbl/
mature /mə'tjʊə/
patient /'peɪʃənt/
rebellious /rɪ'beliəs/
significant /sɪg'nɪfɪkənt/
tolerant /'tɒlərənt/

Verbs

acquire /ə'kwaɪə/
develop /dɪ'veləp/
gesture /'dʒestʃə/
grow /grəʊ/
imitate /'ɪmɪteɪt/
look back
master /'mɑːstə/
mature /mə'tjʊə/
remember /rɪ'membə/
remind /rɪ'maɪnd/
reminisce /ˌremɪ'nɪs/
throw a tantrum
visualise /'vɪʒuəlaɪz/

Adverbs

typically /'tɪpɪkli/

Phrases with mind

bear in mind
broaden the mind
have something in mind /
have something on your mind
it slipped my mind
keep an open mind
my mind went blank
put your mind at ease

UNIT 3

KEEPING FIT

Nouns

allergy /'ælədʒi/
anxiety /æŋ'zaɪəti/
appetite /'æpɪtaɪt/
artery /'ɑːtəri/
asset /'æset/
benefit /'benɪfɪt/
cravings /'kreɪvɪŋz/
depression /dɪ'preʃən/
diagnosis /ˌdaɪəg'nəʊsɪs/
diet /daɪət/
dietician /ˌdaɪə'tɪʃən/
disease /dɪ'ziːz/
(eating) disorder /dɪ'sɔːdə/
exercise /'eksəsaɪz/
factor /'fæktə/
fast food /fɑːst fuːd/
fat /fæt/
harm /hɑːm/
health /helθ/
heart attack /hɑːt ə'tæk/
infection /ɪn'fekʃən/
ingredients /ɪn'griːdiənts/
insomnia /ɪn'sɒmniə/

intake /'ɪnteɪk/
junk food /dʒʌŋk fuːd/
muscle /'mʌsəl/
nutrient /'njuːtriənt/
nutrition /nju:'trɪʃən/
obesity /əʊ'biːsəti/
onset /'ɒnset/
portion /'pɔːʃən/
risk /rɪsk/
serving /'sɜːvɪŋ/
stress /stres/
stroke /strəʊk/
treatment /'triːtmənt/
therapy /'θerəpi/
variety /və'raɪəti/
weight /weɪt/

Adjectives

acute /ə'kjuːt/
allergic /ə'lɜːdʒɪk/
alternate /ɒl'tɜːnət/
brisk /'brɪsk/
chronic /'krɒnɪk/
harmful /'hɑːmfəl/
healthy /'helθi/
infectious /ɪn'fekʃəs/
moderate /'mɒdərət/
obese /əʊ'biːs/
overweight /'əʊvəweɪt/
persistent /pə'sɪstənt/
regular /'regjʊlə/
vital /'vaɪtəl/

Verbs

avoid /ə'vɔɪd/
counteract /ˌkaʊntər'ækt/
curb /kɜːb/
cure /kjʊə/
diminish /dɪ'mɪnɪʃ/
disrupt /dɪs'rʌpt/
eliminate /ɪ'lɪmɪneɪt/
maintain /meɪn'teɪn/
overdo /əʊvə'duː/
overeat /ˌəʊvər'iːt/
prevent /prɪ'vent/
recommend /ˌrekə'mend/
recover /rɪ'kʌvə/
reduce /rɪ'djuːs/
skip /skɪp/
stimulate /'stɪmjəleɪt/
trigger /'trɪgə/

UNIT 4

LIFESTYLES

Nouns
activity /æk'tɪvəti/
aspect /'æspekt/
attitude /'ætɪtjuːd/
(achieve a) balance /'bæləns/
competition /ˌkɒmpə'tɪʃən/
creativity /ˌkriːeɪ'tɪvəti/
daily routine
desire /dɪ'zaɪə/
disappointment /ˌdɪsə'pɔɪntmənt/
experience /ɪk'spɪəriəns/
fulfillment /fʊl'fɪlmənt/
goal /gəʊl/
hobby /'hɒbi/
insight /'ɪnsaɪt/
leisure /'leʒə/
lifestyle /'laɪfstaɪl/
optimist /'ɒptɪmɪst/
outlook /'aʊtlʊk/
opportunity /ˌɒpə'tjuːnəti/
personality /ˌpɜːsən'æləti/
pessimist /'pesɪmɪst/
priority /praɪ'ɒrəti/
pressure /'preʃə/
realist /'rɪəlɪst/
risk-taker /rɪsk 'teɪkə/
self-expression /self ɪk'spreʃən/
sense /sens/

Adjectives
active /'æktɪv/
bored /bɔːd/
confused /kən'fjuːzd/
dissatisfied /dɪs'sætɪsfaɪd/
intense /ɪn'tens/
materialistic /məˌtɪəriə'lɪstɪk/
negative /'negətɪv/
outdoor /aʊt'dɔː/
positive /'pɒzətɪv/
recreational /ˌrekri'eɪʃənəl/
successful /sək'sesfəl/

Verbs
achieve (a goal) /ə'tʃiːv/
appeal /ə'piːl/
attract /ə'trækt/
choose /tʃuːz/
express /ɪk'spres/
enjoy /ɪn'dʒɔɪ/
fulfil /fʊl'fɪl/
improve /ɪm'pruːv/
motivate /'məʊtɪveɪt/
participate /paː'tɪsɪpeɪt/
regret /rɪ'gret/
relax /rɪ'læks/
satisfy /'sætɪsfaɪ/

Verb phrases
lead a happy life
live life on the edge
live life to the full

make a choice
make a decision
make a living
meet a need
miss (an opportunity)
play a role
put pressure on
set (a goal)
take part (in)
work hard for a living

Phrases with life or living
all walks of life
cost of living
lifelong ambition
living expenses
once in a lifetime opportunity
standard of living
way of life

UNIT 5

STUDENT LIFE

Nouns
assignment /ə'saɪnmənt/
college /'kɒlɪdʒ/
controversy /'kɒntrəvɜːsi/
curriculum /kə'rɪkjələm/
dissertation /ˌdɪsə'teɪʃən/
education /ˌedʒʊ'keɪʃən/
exam /ɪg'zæm/
field (of study) /'fiːld/
findings /'faɪndɪŋz/
funding /'fʌndɪŋ/
grade /greɪd/
graduation /ˌgrædʒu'eɪʃən/
grant /graːnt/
high school /haɪ skuːl/
homework /'həʊmwɜːk/
junior school /'dʒuːniə skuːl/
kindergarten /'kɪndəˌgaːtən/
learning disorder
lecturer /'lektʃərə/
library /'laɪbrəri/
limits /'lɪmɪts/
Masters /'maːstəz/
nursery /'nɜːsri/
PhD /ˌpiːeɪtʃ'diː/
primary school /'praɪməri skuːl/
program /'prəʊgræm/
project /'prɒdʒekt/
research /rɪ'sɜːtʃ/
resources /rɪ'zɔːsɪz/
results /rɪ'zʌlts/
scholarship /'skɒləʃɪp/
scope /skəʊp/
secondary school /'sekəndri skuːl/
sources /'sɔːsɪz/
syllabus /'sɪləbəs/
task /taːsk/
theory /'θɪəri/
thesis /'θiːsɪs/

tutor /'tjuːtə/
topic /'tɒpɪk/
university /ˌjuːnɪ'vɜːsəti/

Adjectives
academic /ˌækə'demɪk/
eligible /'elɪdʒəbl/
mixed /'mɪkst/
postgraduate /ˌpəʊs'grædʒuət/
relevant /'reləvənt/
senior /'siːniə/
single-sex /sɪŋgl'seks/
studious /'stjuːdiəs/
work-related /wɜːk rɪ'leɪtɪd/

Verbs
adopt (an approach) /ə'dɒpt/
analyse /'ænəlaɪz/
conduct /'kɒndʌkt/
concentrate /'kɒnsəntreɪt/
consider /kən'sɪdə/
find out /faɪnd aʊt/
graduate /'grædʒuət/
learn (about) /lɜːn/
organise /'ɔːgənaɪz/
overcome /ˌəʊvə'kʌm/
review /rɪ'vjuː/
revise /rɪ'vaɪz/
struggle /'strʌgəl/
take (a course) /teɪk/

Adverbs
relatively /'relətɪvli/

UNIT 6

EFFECTIVE COMMUNICATION

Nouns
accuracy /'ækjərəsi/
communication /kəˌmjuːnɪ'keɪʃən/
concept /'kɒnsept/
conjecture /kən'dʒektʃə/
dialect /'daɪəlekt/
fluency /'fluːənsi/
gesture /'dʒestʃə/
hesitation /ˌhezɪ'teɪʃən/
language /'læŋgwɪdʒ/
language barrier
linguist /'lɪŋgwɪst/
linguistics /lɪŋ'gwɪstɪks/
means of communication
mother tongue
native speaker
pronunciation /prəˌnʌnsi'eɪʃən/
sign language /saɪn 'læŋgwɪdʒ/
vocabulary /və'kæbjələri/

Adjectives
incoherent /ˌɪnkəʊ'hɪərənt/
inherent /ɪn'herənt/
sophisticated /sə'fɪstɪkeɪtɪd/
spontaneous /spɒn'teɪniəs/

Verbs
clarify /'klærɪfaɪ/
communicate /kə'mjuːnɪkeɪt/
comprehend /ˌkɒmprɪ'hend/
conclude /kən'kluːd/
confirm /kən'fɜːm/
converse /'kɒnvɜːs/
define /dɪ'faɪn/
demonstrate /'demənstreɪt/
distinguish /dɪ'stɪŋgwɪʃ/
emerge /ɪ'mɜːdʒ/
evolve /ɪ'vɒlv/
explain /ɪk'spleɪn/
express /ɪk'spres/
gesture /'dʒestʃə/
illustrate /'ɪləstreɪt/
imply /ɪm'plaɪ/
indicate /'ɪndɪkeɪt/
pronounce /prə'naʊns/
recall /rɪ'kɔːl/
refer (to) /rɪ'fɜː/
signify /'sɪgnɪfaɪ/
state /steɪt/
stutter /'stʌtə/
suggest /sə'dʒest/
translate /trænz'leɪt/

Idioms
there is something to be said for
needless to say
have a say
when all is said and done
having said that
to say the least
You can say that again!
that is to say

UNIT 7

ON THE MOVE

Nouns
accommodation /əˌkɒmə'deɪʃən/
attraction /ə'trækʃən/
community /kə'mjuːnəti/
countryside /'kʌntrisaɪd/
destination /ˌdestɪ'neɪʃən/
eco-tourism /'iːkəʊˌtʊərɪzəm/
effect /ɪ'fekt/
facilities /fə'sɪlətiz/
identification /aɪˌdentɪfɪ'keɪʃən/
inhabitant /ɪn'hæbɪtənt/
itinerary /aɪ'tɪnərəri/
journey /'dʒɜːni/
landscape /'lænskeɪp/
luggage /'lʌgɪdʒ/
peak /piːk/
tourism /'tʊərɪzəm/
tourist /'tʊərɪst/
transport /'trænspɔːt/
travel /'trævəl/
travelling /'trævəlɪŋ/
trend /trend/

trip /trɪp/
village /ˈvɪlɪdʒ/

Adjectives
adventurous /ədˈventʃərəs/
budget /ˈbʌdʒɪt/
breathtaking /ˈbreθˌteɪkɪŋ/
coastal /ˈkəʊstəl/
cosmopolitan /ˌkɒzməˈpɒlɪtən/
diverse /daɪˈvɜːs/
flexible /ˈfleksɪbl/
foreign /ˈfɒrɪn/
local /ˈləʊkəl/
luxurious /lʌgˈʒʊəriəs/
mountainous /ˈmaʊntɪnəs/
peaceful /ˈpiːsfəl/
picturesque /ˌpɪktʃərˈesk/
polluted /pəˈluːtɪd/
quaint /kweɪnt/
remote /rɪˈməʊt/
rough /rʌf/
rural /ˈrʊərəl/
scenic /ˈsiːnɪk/
stunning /ˈstʌnɪŋ/
tough /tʌf/
traditional /trəˈdɪʃənəl/
unspoilt /ʌnˈspɔɪlt/
urban /ˈɜːbən/

Verbs
affect /əˈfekt/
fluctuate /ˈflʌktʃueɪt/

UNIT 8

THROUGH THE AGES

Nouns
age /eɪdʒ/
archaeologist /ˌɑːkiˈɒlədʒɪst/
century /ˈsentʃəri/
decade /ˈdekeɪd/
era /ˈɪərə/
evidence /ˈevɪdəns/
excavation /ˌekskəˈveɪʃən/
generation /ˌdʒenəˈreɪʃən/
the Middle Ages
millennia /mɪˈleniə/
period /ˈpɪəriəd/
phase /feɪz/
pioneer /ˌpaɪəˈnɪə/
timeline /ˈtaɪmlaɪn/

Adjectives
ancient /ˈeɪnʃənt/
chronological /ˌkrɒnəˈlɒdʒɪkəl/
consecutive /kənˈsekjʊtɪv/
historical /hɪˈstɒrɪkəl/
imminent /ˈɪmɪnənt/
middle-aged /ˌmɪdəlˈeɪdʒd/
nostalgic /nɒsˈtældʒɪk/
prehistoric /ˌpriːhɪˈstɒrɪk/
prior (to) /praɪə/
punctual /ˈpʌŋktjuəl/
time-consuming
   /ˈtaɪmkənˌsjuːmɪŋ/

Verbs
erode /ɪˈrəʊd/
infer /ɪnˈfɜː/
predate /ˌpriːˈdeɪt/
span /spæn/

Phrases with *time*
in time
lose track of time
on time
save time
spend time
take so long
the right time

Adverbs
chronologically
   /ˌkrɒnəˈlɒdʒɪkəli/
formerly /ˈfɔːməli/
previously /ˈpriːviəsli/
subsequently /ˈsʌbsɪkwəntli/

UNIT 9

THE NATURAL WORLD

Nouns
agriculture /ˈægrɪkʌltʃə/
animal kingdom
burrow /ˈbʌrəʊ/
climate /ˈklaɪmət/
crop(s) /krɒp/
decline /dɪˈklaɪn/
den /den/
disaster /dɪˈzɑːstə/
ecological balance
ecology /iːˈkɒlədʒi/
evolution /ˌiːvəˈluːʃən/
extinction /ɪkˈstɪŋkʃən/
fauna /ˈfɔːnə/
flora /ˈflɔːrə/
genetics /dʒəˈnetɪks/
habitat /ˈhæbɪtæt/
human nature
insect /ˈɪnsekt/
Mother Nature
pesticides /ˈpestɪsaɪdz/
predator /ˈpredətə/
prey /preɪ/
repercussions /ˌriːpəˈkʌʃənz/
scent /sent/
species /ˈspiːʃiːz/
soil /sɔɪl/
vegetation /ˌvedʒɪˈteɪʃən/
vermin /ˈvɜːmɪn/
weed /wiːd/

Adjectives
arid /ˈærɪd/
catastrophic /ˌkætəˈstrɒfɪk/
disastrous /dɪˈzɑːstrəs/
domesticated /dəˈmestɪkeɪtɪd/
endangered /ɪnˈdeɪndʒəd/
extinct /ɪkˈstɪŋkt/
genetically-modified

introduced /ˌɪntrəˈdjuːst/
native /ˈneɪtɪv/
natural /ˈnætʃərəl/
resistant /rɪˈzɪstənt/
semi-arid /ˈsemi ˈærɪd/
tropical /ˈtrɒpɪkəl/
vulnerable /ˈvʌlnərəbəl/
wild /waɪld/

Verbs
adapt /əˈdæpt/
combat /ˈkɒmbæt/
cultivate /ˈkʌltɪveɪt/
eradicate /ɪˈrædɪkeɪt/
evolve /ɪˈvɒlv/
hibernate /ˈhaɪbəneɪt/
tolerate /ˈtɒləreɪt/

UNIT 10

REACHING FOR THE SKIES

Nouns
asteroid /ˈæstərɔɪd/
astronaut /ˈæstrənɔːt/
atmosphere /ˈætməsfɪə/
cosmos /ˈkɒzmɒs/
crater /ˈkreɪtə/
debris /ˈdeɪbriː/
Earth /ɜːθ/
exploration /ˌekspləˈreɪʃən/
explorer /ɪkˈsplɔːrə/
galaxy /ˈgæləksi/
gas /gæs/
gravity /ˈgrævəti/
horizon /həˈraɪzən/
launch /lɔːnʃ/
meteor /ˈmiːtiə/
moon /muːn/
ocean /ˈəʊʃən/
orbit /ˈɔːbɪt/
outer space /ˈaʊtə speɪs/
planet /ˈplænɪt/
radiation /ˌreɪdiˈeɪʃən/
rocket /ˈrɒkɪt/
satellite /ˈsætəlaɪt/
simulator /ˈsɪmjəleɪtə/
solar system /ˈsəʊlə ˈsɪstəm/
space /speɪs/
spacecraft /ˈspeɪskrɑːft/
space shuttle /speɪs ˈʃʌtəl/
space station /speɪs ˈsteɪʃən/
surface /ˈsɜːfɪs/
universe /ˈjuːnɪvɜːs/
weightlessness /ˈweɪtləsnəs/

Adjectives
commercial /kəˈmɜːʃəl/
cosmic /ˈkɒzmɪk/
extreme /ɪkˈstriːm/
gravitational /ˌgrævɪˈteɪʃənəl/
horizontal /ˌhɒrɪˈzɒntəl/
inevitable /ɪˈnevɪtəbl/
lunar /ˈluːnə/

meteoric /ˌmiːtiˈɒrɪk/
outer /ˈaʊtə/
solar /ˈsəʊlə/
terrestrial /təˈrestriəl/
toxic /ˈtɒksɪk/
uninhabitable /ˌʌnɪnˈhæbɪtəbl/
universal /ˌjuːnɪˈvɜːsəl/
unmanned /ʌnˈmænd/

Verbs
acclimatise /əˈklaɪmətaɪz/
colonise /ˈkɒlənaɪz/
explore /ɪkˈsplɔː/
float /fləʊt/
orbit /ˈɔːbɪt/
propel /prəˈpel/
rotate /rəˈteɪt/
sustain /səˈsteɪn/
simulate /ˈsɪmjəleɪt/
undergo /ˌʌndəˈgəʊ/

UNIT 11

DESIGN AND INNOVATION

Nouns
balcony /ˈbælkəni/
brick /brɪk/
building /ˈbɪldɪŋ/
ceiling /ˈsiːlɪŋ/
concrete /ˈkɒŋkriːt/
construction /kənˈstrʌkʃən/
cottage /ˈkɒtɪdʒ/
design /dɪˈzaɪn/
device /dɪˈvaɪs/
elevator /ˈelɪveɪtə/
engineering /ˌendʒɪˈnɪərɪŋ/
frame /freɪm/
gadget /ˈgædʒɪt/
housing /ˈhaʊzɪŋ/
innovation /ˌɪnəˈveɪʃən/
invention /ɪnˈvenʃən/
landmark /ˈlændmɑːk/
lift shaft /lɪft ʃɑːft/
occupant /ˈɒkjəpənt/
platform /ˈplætfɔːm/
quarry /ˈkwɒri/
residence /ˈrezɪdəns/
skyscraper /ˈskaɪˌskreɪpə/
staircase /ˈsteəkeɪs/
steel /stiːl/
storage /ˈstɔːrɪdʒ/
structure /ˈstrʌktʃə/
tension /ˈtenʃən/
timber /ˈtɪmbə/

Adjectives
airy /ˈeəri/
conventional /kənˈvenʃənəl/
cosy /ˈkəʊzi/
cramped /kræmpt/
curved /kɜːvd/
disposable /dɪˈspəʊzəbl/
domestic /dəˈmestɪk/

exterior /ɪkˈstɪəriə/
functional /ˈfʌŋkʃənəl/
futuristic /ˌfjuːtʃəˈrɪstɪk/
high-rise /ˌhaɪˈraɪz/
innovative /ˈɪnəvətɪv/
internal /ɪnˈtɜːnəl/
mass-produced /ˌmæsprəˈdjuːst/
modern /ˈmɒdən/
multi-storey /ˌmʌltiˈstɔːri/
old-fashioned /ˌəʊlˈfæʃənd/
ornate /ɔːˈneɪt/
prefabricated /ˌpriːˈfæbrɪkeɪtɪd/
single-storey /ˈsɪŋɡəl ˈstɔːri/
spacious /ˈspeɪʃəs/
state-of-the-art
traditional /trəˈdɪʃənəl/
two-storey /tuː ˈstɔːri/
typical /ˈtɪpɪkəl/
ultra-modern /ˈʌltrə ˈmɒdən/

Verbs
activate /ˈæktɪveɪt/
automate /ˈɔːtəmeɪt/
build /bɪld/
condemn /kənˈdem/
construct /ˈkənstrʌkt/
decorate /ˈdekəreɪt/
demolish /dɪˈmɒlɪʃ/
design /dɪˈzaɪn/
develop /dɪˈveləp/
devise /dɪˈvaɪz/
haul /hɔːl/
hoist /hɔɪst/
invent /ɪnˈvent/
maintain /meɪnˈteɪn/
occupy /ˈɒkjəpaɪ/
reconstruct /ˌriːkənˈstrʌkt/
renovate /ˈrenəveɪt/
support /səˈpɔːt/
trigger /ˈtrɪɡə/

UNIT 12

INFORMATION TECHNOLOGY

Nouns
automatic pilot
computerisation
  /kəmˌpjuːtəraɪˈzeɪʃən/
connection /kəˈnekʃən/
data /ˈdeɪtə/
device /dɪˈvaɪs/
function /ˈfʌŋkʃən/
gadget /ˈɡædʒɪt/
the Internet
keyboard /ˈkiːbɔːd/
keypad /ˈkiːpæd/
laptop (computer) /ˈlæptɒp/
the latest
memory /ˈmeməri/
monitor /ˈmɒnɪtə/
patent /ˈpeɪtənt/
program /ˈprəʊɡræm/

prototype /ˈprəʊtətaɪp/
remote control /rɪˈməʊt
  kənˈtrəʊl/
silicon chip /ˈsɪlɪkən tʃɪp/
technology /tekˈnɒlədʒi/
telecommunications
  /ˌtelɪkəˌmjuːnɪˈkeɪʃənz/
vision /ˈvɪʒən/
wireless connection

Adjectives
compact /ˈkɒmpækt/
computerised
  /kəmˈpjuːtəraɪzd/
cutting-edge /ˈkʌtɪŋedʒ/
cyber /ˈsaɪbə/
dated /ˈdeɪtɪd/
digital /ˈdɪdʒɪtəl/
labour-saving /ˈleɪbəˌseɪvɪŋ/
portable /ˈpɔːtəbl/
state-of-the-art
up-to-date /ʌptəˈdeɪt/
user-friendly /ˌjuːzəˈfrendli/
virtual /ˈvɜːtʃuəl/
wireless connection

Verbs
access /ˈækses/
connect /kəˈnekt/
download /ˌdaʊnˈləʊd/
display /dɪˈspleɪ/
envisage /ɪnˈvɪzɪdʒ/
operate /ˈɒpəreɪt/
revolutionise /ˌrevəˈluːʃənaɪz/
scroll /skrəʊl/
speculate /ˈspekjʊleɪt/
store /stɔː/
surpass /səˈpɑːs/

Adverbs
automatically /ˌɔːtəˈmætɪkli/

UNIT 13

THE MODERN WORLD

Nouns
attitude /ˈætɪtjuːd/
brand /brænd/
culture /ˈkʌltʃə/
cycle /ˈsaɪkəl/
demographics
  /ˌdeməʊˈɡræfɪks/
development /dɪˈveləpmənt/
diversity /daɪˈvɜːsəti/
globalisation /ˌɡləʊbəlaɪˈzeɪʃən/
hindsight /ˈhaɪndsaɪt/
icon /ˈaɪkɒn/
identity /aɪˈdentəti/
implication /ˌɪmplɪˈkeɪʃən/
impact /ˈɪmpækt/
increase /ˈɪnkriːs/
influence /ˈɪnfluəns/
industry /ˈɪndəstri/
isolation /ˌaɪsəˈleɪʃən/
joint venture

(have a) monopoly /məˈnɒpəli/
market /ˈmɑːkɪt/
modernisation
  /ˌmɒdənaɪˈzeɪʃən/
multiculturalism
  /ˌmʌltiˈkʌltʃərəlɪzəm/
percentage /pəˈsentɪdʒ/
population /ˌpɒpjʊˈleɪʃən/
prediction /prɪˈdɪkʃən/
projection /prəˈdʒekʃən/
proportion /prəˈpɔːʃən/
rate /reɪt/
statistics /stəˈtɪstɪks/
trend /trend/

Adjectives
ageing /ˈeɪdʒɪŋ/
current /ˈkʌrənt/
demographic /ˌdeməˈɡræfɪk/
elderly /ˈeldəli/
ethnic /ˈeθnɪk/
exotic /ɪɡˈzɒtɪk/
global /ˈɡləʊbəl/
local /ˈləʊkəl/
long-term /lɒŋˈtɜːm/
mid-term /ˌmɪdˈtɜːm/
multicultural /ˌmʌltiˈkʌltʃərəl/
productive /prəˈdʌktɪv/
sceptical /ˈskeptɪkəl/
short-term /ʃɔːtˈtɜːm/
subsequent /ˈsʌbsɪkwənt/
wealthy /ˈwelθi/
worldwide /ˌwɜːldˈwaɪd/

Verbs
compound /ˈkʌmpaʊnd/
contribute /kənˈtrɪbjuːt/
decline /dɪˈklaɪn/
diminish /dɪˈmɪnɪʃ/
dominate /ˈdɒmɪneɪt/
dwindle /ˈdwɪndəl/
factor /ˈfæktə/
indicate /ˈɪndɪkeɪt/
merge /mɜːdʒ/
migrate /maɪˈɡreɪt/

UNIT 14

URBANISATION

Nouns
benefit /ˈbenɪfɪt/
challenge /ˈtʃælɪndʒ/
compromise /ˈkɒmprəmaɪz/
difficulty /ˈdɪfɪkəlti/
dilemma /dɪˈlemə/
inhabitant /ɪnˈhæbɪtənt/
infrastructure /ˈɪnfrəˌstrʌktʃə/
isolation /ˌaɪsəˈleɪʃən/
issue /ˈɪʃuː/
megacity /ˈmeɡəsɪti/
migrant /ˈmaɪɡrənt/
obstacle /ˈɒbstəkəl/
overpopulation
  /ˌəʊvəˌpɒpjʊˈleɪʃən/

population /ˌpɒpjʊˈleɪʃən/
poverty /ˈpɒvəti/
resolution /ˌrezəˈluːʃən/
setback /ˈsetbæk/
slum /slʌm/
solution /səˈluːʃən/
tolerance /ˈtɒlərəns/
traffic /ˈtræfɪk/
urbanisation /ɜːbənaɪˈzeɪʃən/

Adjectives
adequate /ˈædɪkwət/
basic /ˈbeɪsɪk/
booming /ˈbuːmɪŋ/
catastrophic /ˌkætəˈstrɒfɪk/
crowded /ˈkraʊdɪd/
decent /ˈdiːsənt/
developing /dɪˈveləpɪŋ/
double-edged /dʌblˈedʒd/
isolated /ˈaɪsəleɪtɪd/
one-sided /wɒn ˈsaɪdɪd/
long-sighted /lɒŋˈsaɪtɪd/
long-term /ˌlɒŋˈtɜːm/
overpriced /ˌəʊvəˈpraɪst/
overworked /ˌəʊvəˈwɜːkt/
pressing /ˈpresɪŋ/
rural /ˈrʊərəl/
short-sighted /ʃɔːt ˈsaɪtɪd/
short-term /ˌʃɔːtˈtɜːm/
staggering /ˈstæɡərɪŋ/
tolerant /ˈtɒlərənt/

Verbs
address /əˈdres/
adjust /əˈdʒʌst/
aggravate /ˈæɡrəveɪt/
cause /kɔːz/
compete /kəmˈpiːt/
compound /ˈkʌmpaʊnd/
deal with
deteriorate /dɪˈtɪəriəreɪt/
enhance /ɪnˈhɑːns/
exacerbate /ɪɡˈzæsəbeɪt/
exclude /ɪksˈkluːd/
face /feɪs/
flourish /ˈflʌrɪʃ/
identify /aɪˈdentɪfaɪ/
improve /ɪmˈpruːv/
include /ɪnˈkluːd/
linger /ˈlɪŋɡə/
modify /ˈmɒdɪfaɪ/
overcome /ˌəʊvəˈkʌm/
present /ˈprezˈənt/
raise /reɪz/
reform /rɪˈfɔːm/
regulate /ˈreɡjʊleɪt/
remedy /ˈremədi/
resolve /rɪˈzɒlv/
tackle /ˈtækəl/
tolerate /ˈtɒləreɪt/
transform /trænsˈfɔːm/
worsen /ˈwɜːsən/

Verb phrases
find a solution
overcome a difficulty

reach/find a compromise
remedy a situation
resolve an issue

UNIT 15

THE GREEN REVOLUTION

Nouns
acid rain /'æsɪd reɪn/
biodiversity /ˌbaɪəʊdaɪ'vɜːsəti/
climate change
contamination
    /kən,tæmɪ'neɪʃən/
deforestation /diːˌfɒrɪ'steɪʃən/
disposal /dɪ'spəʊzəl/
drought /draʊt/
ecosystem /'iːkəʊˌsɪstəm/
emission /ɪ'mɪʃən/
the environment
erosion /ɪ'rəʊʒən/
exhaust (fumes) /ɪg'zɔːst/
fertilizer /'fɜːtɪlaɪzə/
flood /flʌd/
food chain /fuːd tʃeɪn/
fumes /fjuːmz/
greenhouse gases
impact /'ɪmpækt/
pollutant /pə'luːtənt/
pollution /pə'luːʃən/
process /'prəʊses/
refuse /'refjuːs/
strain /streɪn/
threat /θret/
waste /weɪst/

Adjectives
achievable /ə'tʃiːvəbl/
advantageous /ˌædvən'teɪdʒəs/
at risk /æt rɪsk/
beneficial /ˌbenɪ'fɪʃəl/
chronic /'krɒnɪk/
conceivable /kən'siːvəbl/
contaminated /kən'tæmɪneɪtɪd/
devastating /'devəsteɪtɪŋ/
doubtful /'daʊtfəl/
environmental
    /ɪn,vaɪrən'mentəl/
environmentally friendly
feasible /'fiːzəbl/
fruitless /'fruːtləs/
futile /'fjuːtaɪl/
immune /ɪ'mjuːn/
impracticable /ɪm'præktɪkəbl/
improbable /ɪm'prɒbəbl/
in danger (of)
insoluble /ɪn'sɒljəbl/
irreparable /ɪ'reprəbl/
irreplaceable /ˌɪrɪ'pleɪsəbl/
irreversible /ˌɪrɪ'vɜːsəbl/
liable /'laɪəbl/
life-threatening /'laɪf,θretənɪŋ/
pervasive /pə'veɪsɪv/
pointless /'pɔɪntləs/

pristine /'prɪstiːn/
questionable /'kwestʃənəbl/
recyclable /ˌriː'saɪkləbl/
sustainable /sə'steɪnəbl/
taxing /'tæksɪŋ/
unattainable /ˌʌnə'teɪnəbl/
unlikely /ʌn'laɪkli/
unprecedented /ʌn'presɪdəntɪd/
useless /'juːsləs/
viable /'vaɪəbl/
vital /'vaɪtəl/
worthwhile /ˌwɜːθ'waɪl/

Verbs
confront /kən'frʌnt/
contaminate /kən'tæmɪneɪt/
dispose of
dump /dʌmp/
threaten /'θretən/

Adverbs
inexorably /ɪ'neksərəbli/
inevitably /ɪ'nevɪtəbli/

UNIT 16

THE ENERGY CRISIS

Nouns
atmosphere /'ætməsfɪə/
balance /'bæləns/
biofuel /baɪəʊfjʊəl/
carbon /'kɑːbən/
carbon dioxide /'kɑːbən
    daɪ'ɒksaɪd/
crisis /'kraɪsɪs/
electricity /ˌɪlek'trɪsɪti/
emissions /ɪ'mɪʃənz/
exhaust /ɪg'zɔːst/
fossil fuel /'fɒsəl 'fjuːəl/
fuel /'fjuːəl/
fumes /fjuːmz/
gas /gæs/
greenhouse gas /'griːnhaʊs gæs/
hybrid /'haɪbrɪd/
hydrogen /'haɪdrədʒən/
petrol /'petrəl/
resources /rɪ'zɔːsɪz/
turbine /'tɜːbaɪn/
vehicle /'vɪəkəl/

Adjectives
alternative /ɒl'tɜːnətɪv/
critical /'krɪtɪkəl/
disposable /dɪ'spəʊzəbl/
drastic /'dræstɪk/
eco-friendly /'iːkəʊ,frendli/
efficient /ɪ'fɪʃənt/
effective /ɪ'fektɪv/
environmentally friendly
nuclear /'njuːkliə/
rechargeable /riː'tʃɑːdʒəbl/
renewable /rɪ'njuːəbəl/
solar /'səʊlə/
unleaded (petrol) /ʌn'ledɪd/

Verbs
absorb /əb'zɔːb/
conserve /kən'sɜːv/
consume /kən'sjuːm/
convert /'kʌnvɜːt/
counter /'kaʊntə/
deplete /dɪ'pliːt/
diminish /dɪ'mɪnɪʃ/
discharge /'dɪstʃɑːdʒ/
dwindle /'dwɪndəl/
emit /ɪ'mɪt/
expend /ɪk'spend/
limit /'lɪmɪt/
maintain /meɪn'teɪn/
outweigh /ˌaʊt'weɪ/
preserve /prɪ'zɜːv/
retain /rɪ'teɪn/
waste /weɪst/

UNIT 17

TALKING BUSINESS

Nouns
advertisement /əd'vɜːtɪsmənt/
advertising /'ædvətaɪzɪŋ/
boss /bɒs/
campaign /kæm'peɪn/
candidate /'kændɪdət/
career /kə'rɪə/
clerk /klɑːk/
client /klaɪənt/
colleague /'kɒliːg/
company /'kʌmpəni/
consumer /kən'sjuːmə/
credibility /ˌkredə'bɪləti/
customer /'kʌstəmə/
earnings /'ɜːnɪŋz/
employee /ɪm'plɔɪiː/
employer /ɪm'plɔɪə/
employment /ɪm'plɔɪmənt/
experience /ɪk'spɪəriəns/
goods /gʊdz/
income /'ɪnkʌm/
industry /'ɪndəstri/
interview /'ɪntəvjuː/
job /dʒɒb/
job satisfaction
labourer /'leɪbərə/
management /'mænɪdʒmənt/
manual work /'mænjuəl wɜːk/
market /'mɑːkɪt/
marketing /'mɑːkɪtɪŋ/
meeting /'miːtɪŋ/
money /'mʌni/
niche /niːʃ/
occupation /ˌɒkjə'peɪʃən/
office /'ɒfɪs/
overtime /'əʊvətaɪm/
packaging /'pækɪdʒɪŋ/
pay /peɪ/
perk /pɜːk/
product /'prɒdʌkt/
profession /prə'feʃən/

prospects /'prɒspekts/
qualifications /ˌkwɒlɪfɪ'keɪʃənz/
retirement /rɪ'taɪəmənt/
salary /'sæləri/
shares /ʃeəz/
shift work /ʃɪft wɜːk/
skills /skɪlz/
staff /stɑːf/
supervisor /'suːpəvaɪzə/
takeover /'teɪkˌəʊvə/
target /'tɑːgɪt/
trade /treɪd/
trend /trend/
unemployment /ˌʌnɪm'plɔɪmənt/
wages /'weɪdʒɪz/
workforce /'wɜːkfɔːs/
workplace /'wɜːkpleɪs/

Adjectives
casual /'kæʒjuəl/
demanding /dɪ'mɑːndɪŋ/
economic /ˌiːkə'nɒmɪk/
economical /ˌiːkə'nɒmɪkəl/
exhausting /ɪg'zɔːstɪŋ/
hospitality /ˌhɒspɪ'tæləti/
monotonous /mə'nɒtənəs/
part-time /ˌpɑːt'taɪm/
retail /'riːteɪl/
redundant /rɪ'dʌndənt/
rewarding /rɪ'wɔːdɪŋ/
unemployed /ˌʌnɪm'plɔɪd/
unskilled /ʌn'skɪld/

Verbs
apply /ə'plaɪ/
compete /kəm'piːt/
earn /ɜːn/
endorse /ɪn'dɔːs/
invest (in) /ɪn'vest/
persuade /pə'sweɪd/
to be promoted
request /rɪ'kwest/
retire /rɪ'taɪə/

UNIT 18

THE LAW

Nouns
actions /'ækʃənz/
arson /'ɑːsən/
authority /ɔː'θɒrəti/
burglary /'bɜːgləri/
consequences /'kɒntsɪkwəntsɪz/
convict /'kɒnvɪkt/
crime /kraɪm/
crime rate /kraɪm reɪt/
criminal /'krɪmɪnəl/
deterrent /dɪ'terənt/
evidence /'evɪdəns/
fine /faɪn/
fraud /frɔːd/
imprisonment /ɪm'prɪzənmənt/
inequality /ˌɪnɪ'kwɒləti/
intent /ɪn'tent/

intrusion /ɪn'truːʒən/
judge /dʒʌdʒ/
jury /'dʒʊəri/
kidnapping /'kɪdnæpɪŋ/
lawyer /'lɔɪə/
motive /'məʊtɪv/
murder /'mɜːdə/
offence /ə'fens/
pickpocketing /'pɪkpɒkɪtɪŋ/
prevention /prɪ'venʃən/
prison /'prɪzən/
prisoner /'prɪzənə/
property crime /'prɒpəti kraɪm/
prosecutor /'prɒsɪkjuːtə/
protection /prə'tekʃən/
punishment /'pʌnɪʃmənt/
recklessness /'rekləsnəs/
smuggling /'smʌglɪŋ/
social system /'səʊʃəl 'sɪstəm/
swearing /'sweərɪŋ/
the accused
toxic waste /'tɒksɪk weɪst/
vandalism /'vændəlɪzəm/
victim /'vɪktɪm/
violation /ˌvaɪə'leɪʃən/

Adjectives

criminal /'krɪmɪnəl/
drug-related /drʌg rɪ'leɪtɪd/
evil /'iːvəl/
guilty /'gɪlti/
harsh /hɑːʃ/
innocent /'ɪnəsənt/
intentional /ɪn'tenʃənəl/
law-abiding /'lɔːəˌbaɪdɪŋ/
non-violent /ˌnɒn'vaɪələnt/
offensive /ə'fensɪv/
on trial /ɒn traɪəl/
petty (crime) /'peti/
punishable /'pʌnɪʃəbl/
random /'rændəm/
strict /strɪkt/
unintentional /ˌʌnɪn'tenʃənəl/
victimless /'vɪktɪmləs/

Verbs

abide (by) /ə'baɪd/
abolish /ə'bɒlɪʃ/
combat /'kɒmbæt/
deter /dɪ'tɜː/
enforce /ɪn'fɔːs/
imprison /ɪm'prɪzən/
monitor /'mɒnɪtə/
obey /ə'beɪ/
offend /ə'fend/
perpetrate /'pɜːpɪtreɪt/
prevent /prɪ'vent/
protect /prə'tekt/
prove /pruːv/
punish /'pʌnɪʃ/
resent /rɪ'zent/
respect /rɪ'spekt/
violate /'vaɪəleɪt/

Verb phrases

accept the consequences
commit a crime
convict a criminal
impose a fine
pass a law
solve a crime

UNIT 19

THE MEDIA

Nouns

access /'ækses/
attitude /'ætɪtjuːd/
author /'ɔːθə/
bias /'baɪəs/
censorship /'sensəʃɪp/
challenge /'tʃælɪndʒ/
credibility /ˌkredə'bɪləti/
current affairs /'kʌrənt ə'feəz/
editor /'edɪtə/
exposé /ek'spəʊzeɪ/
exposure /ɪk'spəʊʒə/
fame /feɪm/
free press /friː pres/
ideology /ˌaɪdi'ɒlədʒi/
influence /'ɪnfluəns/
the Internet
investigation /ɪnˌvestɪ'geɪʃən/
issue /'ɪʃuː/
journal /'dʒɜːnəl/
journalism /'dʒɜːnəlɪzəm/
mass media /mæs 'miːdiə/
media /'miːdiə/
network /'netwɜːk/
the news
newspaper /'njuːsˌpeɪpə/
newsstand /'njuːzstænd/
opinion /ə'pɪnjən/
paparazzi /ˌpæpə'rætsi/
press /pres/
privacy /'prɪvəsi/
publication /ˌpʌblɪ'keɪʃən/
publicity /pʌb'lɪsəti/
publisher /'pʌblɪʃə/
relevance /'reləvəns/
safeguard /'seɪfgɑːd/
source /sɔːs/
speculation /ˌspekjə'leɪʃən/
tabloid /'tæblɔɪd/
the Web

Adjectives

alternative /ɒl'tɜːnətɪv/
artificial /ˌɑːtɪ'fɪʃəl/
attention-grabbing /ə'tenʃən 'græbɪŋ/
biased /'baɪəst/
celebrity /sə'lebrəti/
controversial /ˌkɒntrə'vɜːʃəl/
distorted /dɪ'stɔːtɪd/
entertaining /ˌentə'teɪnɪŋ/
factual /'fæktʃuəl/

informative /ɪn'fɔːmətɪv/
intrusive /ɪn'truːsɪv/
investigative /ɪn'vestɪgətɪv/
mainstream /'meɪnstriːm/
pervasive /pə'veɪsɪv/
realistic /ˌrɪə'lɪstɪk/
sensationalist /sen'seɪʃənəlɪst/
superficial /ˌsuːpə'fɪʃəl/
unbiased /ʌn'baɪəst/
well-informed /ˌwelɪn'fɔːmd/

Verbs

affect /ə'fekt/
broadcast /'brɔːdkɑːst/
censor /'sensə/
control /kən'trəʊl/
exploit /'eksplɔɪt/
expose /ɪk'spəʊz/
inform /ɪn'fɔːm/
intrude /ɪn'truːd/
invade /ɪn'veɪd/
investigate /ɪn'vestɪgeɪt/
publicize /'pʌblɪsaɪz/
publish /'pʌblɪʃ/
report /rɪ'pɔːt/
review /rɪ'vjuː/
verify /'verɪfaɪ/

UNIT 20

THE ARTS

Nouns

actor /'æktə/
actress /'æktrəs/
aesthetics /iːs'θetɪks/
appreciation /əˌpriːʃi'eɪʃən/
artefact /'ɑːtɪfækt/
artist /'ɑːtɪst/
atmosphere /'ætməsfɪə/
audience /'ɔːdiəns/
ballerina /ˌbælə'riːnə/
ballet /'bæleɪ/
carving /'kɑːvɪŋ/
conception /kən'sepʃən/
concert /'kɒnsət/
crafts /krɑːfts/
creation /kri'eɪʃən/
culture /'kʌltʃə/
emotion /ɪ'məʊʃən/
exhibition /ˌeksɪ'bɪʃən/
expression /ɪk'spreʃən/
festival /'festɪvəl/
gallery /'gæləri/
image /'ɪmɪdʒ/
imagination /ɪˌmædʒɪ'neɪʃən/
influence /'ɪnfluəns/
inspiration /ˌɪnspɪ'reɪʃən/
intimacy /'ɪntɪməsi/
literature /'lɪtrətʃə/
mood /muːd/
musician /mjuː'zɪʃən/
opera /'ɒpərə/
orchestra /'ɔːkɪstrə/

painting /'peɪntɪŋ/
performance /pə'fɔːməns/
the performing arts
play /pleɪ/
portrait /'pɔːtreɪt/
proportion /prə'pɔːʃən/
reflection /rɪ'flekʃən/
response /rɪ'spɒns/
sculptor /'skʌlptə/
sculpture /'skʌlptʃə/
stimulus /'stɪmjələs/
style /staɪl/
taste /teɪst/
theatre /'θɪətə/
theme /θiːm/
venue /'venjuː/
works /wɜːks/
writer /'raɪtə/

Adjectives

abstract /'æbstrækt/
accomplished /ə'kʌmplɪʃt/
aesthetic /iːs'θetɪk/
burgeoning /'bɜːdʒənɪŋ/
classical /'klæsɪkəl/
creative /kri'eɪtɪv/
cultural /'kʌltʃərəl/
distracting /dɪ'stræktɪŋ/
eclectic /ek'lektɪk/
electric /ɪ'lektrɪk/
emotional /ɪ'məʊʃənəl/
fundamental /ˌfʌndə'mentəl/
imaginative /ɪ'mædʒɪnətɪv/
influential /ˌɪnflu'enʃəl/
inspirational /ˌɪnspɪ'reɪʃənəl/
interactive /ˌɪntə'æktɪv/
literary /'lɪtərəri/
live /laɪv/
magical /'mædʒɪkəl/
monotonous /mə'nɒtənəs/
mundane /mʌn'deɪn/
passionate /'pæʃənət/
popular /'pɒpjələ/
prominent /'prɒmɪnənt/
relaxing /rɪ'læksɪŋ/
stimulating /'stɪmjəleɪtɪŋ/
visual /'vɪʒuəl/
vivid /'vɪvɪd/

Verbs

choreograph /'kɒriəgrɑːf/
create /kri'eɪt/
depict /dɪ'pɪkt/
enrich /ɪn'rɪtʃ/
escape /ɪ'skeɪp/
imagine /ɪ'mædʒɪn/
influence /'ɪnfluəns/
inspire /ɪn'spaɪə/
participate /pɑː'tɪsɪpeɪt/
perform /pə'fɔːm/
provoke /prə'vəʊk/
transcend /træn'send/

Acknowledgements

My thanks go to Martine Walsh for commissioning this project, Caroline Thiriau for overseeing it and to my editor, Christine Barton. Geographically, we couldn't have been much further away from each other but all three have helped to make the writing of this book a pleasure. I'm particularly grateful that Christine found enough 'slips' to make me feel confident in the contents of the book and not so many as to make me feel insecure!

Thanks also to Alex (7) and Fraser (9) for their contributions to 'Mum's words'. Alex suggested the word 'harsh' for Unit 18 and Fraser's current favourite word 'random' also made it into the same unit!

Pauline Cullen

The author and publishers are grateful to the following reviewers for their valuable insights and suggestions:
Sean Choi, South Korea; Anthony Cosgrove, UK; Maria Heron, UK; Julie King, UK; David Larbalestier, Australia; Simon Raw, UK

The authors and publishers acknowledge the following sources of copyright material and are grateful for the permissions granted. While every effort has been made, it has not always been possible to identify the sources of all the material used, or to trace all copyright holders. If any omissions are brought to our notice, we will be happy to include the appropriate acknowledgements on reprinting.

pp. 19-20: Adam for adapted text 'Stress' from www.adam.about.com; p. 23: Science Daily LLC for the article adapted from 'UF researcher leisure activities defy simple classifications' by Cathy Keen, from Science Daily, www.sciencedaily.com; p. 33: The Economist for the adapted article 'Signs of Success' 19 February 2004, © The Economist Newspaper Limited; pp. 35-36: Australian Museum for article 'First words: let's stick together' by Richard Fullagar, Nature Australia, Autumn 2004, © Australian Museum 2006; pp. 49-50: National Wildlife Federation for text adapted from 'Meet the hedgehog' by Lisa W Drew, June/July 2005, www.nwf.org; p. 59: Luna Media for adapted text 'The elevator. Going up...' from Cosmos Magazine, July 2005, and for pp. 102: for text adapted from 'Brain of the beholder' by David Sokol, Cosmos Magazine, February/March 2007, © Luna Media Pty Ltd, all rights reserved; pp 61-63: for the article adapted from 'The home of the future, then and now' by Sheryl N Hamilton, Canadian Home Economics Journal, March 2003, © 2007 CNET Networks Inc; p. 65: for the adapted article '2026: A vision for the nation's future – part 2' from The Australian Supplementary Magazine, Copyright 2007 News Limited; p. 69: for text and graph 'Mind the globalization gap' from www.brw.com.au © Business Review Weekly; p. 75-76: Media UK for the adapted article 'Rags, bones and recycling bins' by Tim Cooper, History Today, February 2006; p. 94: Thomson Learning for the adapted text, 'Crime' from The World of Sociology, by Gale, © 2002 The Gale Group; pp. 105-106: Dr Tom Sjöblom, University of Helsinki, for the article 'Storytelling – Narratives of the mind'; p. 112: for the text extracts for the word 'choice' from Cambridge Advanced Learner's Dictionary, 2005, Cambridge University Press; p. 119: US Environmental Protection Agency for the graph, 'National Recycling Rates, 1960 – 2005', www.epa.gov.

The publishers are grateful to the following for permission to reproduce copyright photographs and material:

Key: l = left, c = centre, r = right, t = top, b = bottom

Alamy/©Digital Japan Archive for p23 (r), /©Skyscan Photolibrary for p43, /©BAE Inc for p52, /©Image State for p49, /©Phil Crow for p73, /©Semen Lihodeev for p102 (2), /©Vehbi Koca for p102 (4), /©Charles Mistral for p102 (7); Corbis Images/©Bettmann for p59, /©The Gallery Collection for p102 (1); Getty Images/©Stone for p65, /©Hulton Archive for p102 (3), /©Photographers Choice for p102 (6); Photolibrary for p47; Punchstock/©IT Stock for p23 (l), /©Comstock for p102 (5); Rex Features for pp72, 98, 99; Science & Society PL/Science Museum for p64; Shutterstock/©WizData, Inc for p38.

Picture research: Hilary Luckcock

Text design and page make-up: Kamae Design, Oxford

Concept design: David Lawton

Illustrations: Robert Calow, Mark Duffin, Karen Donnelly, Dylan Gibson, Julian Mosedale, Roger Penwill